What Is Philosophy?

What Is Philosophy?

Edited by C. P. Ragland and Sarah Heidt

Yale University Press   New Haven & London

Published with assistance from the Ernst Cassirer Publications Fund.

Designed by Sonia L. Shannon Set in Bulmer type by Keystone Typesetting, Orwigsburg, Penn.

Printed in the United States of America by Vail-Ballou Press, Binghamton, N.Y.

Library of Congress Cataloging-in-Publication Data What is philosophy? / edited by C. P. Ragland and Sarah Heidt.

p.   cm.

Includes bibliographical references and index.

ISBN 0-300-08755-1 (cloth : alk. paper) — ISBN 0-300-08794-2 (pbk.: alk. paper)

1. Philosophy. I. Ragland, C. P., 1970– II. Heidt, Sarah L., 1968– III. Title.

B29.W45 2001

100—dc21

00-012597

Contents

6
What Is Philosophy?
The Philosophical Point of View After the
End of Dogmatic Metaphysics   153
Karl-Otto Apel

Acknowledgments

In addition to the contributors themselves, many people worked to make this volume possible. The editors would especially like to thank Robert M. Adams, who advised us throughout the project, from its origins as an idea to its final realization in both a conference and a volume; Michael Della Rocca and Allen Wood, who read and commented on an earlier draft of the introduction; and Charles Grench, Otto Bohlmann, Heidi Downey, and Nancy Moore Brochin at Yale University Press, who patiently guided us (as neophyte editors) through the whole editorial process. We are also grateful to the Ernst Cassirer fund at Yale University for support of the original conference.

Introduction
The Act of Philosophizing
C. P. Ragland and Sarah Heidt

"We cannot learn philosophy; for where is it, who is in possession of it, and how shall we recognize it? We can only learn to philosophize."
—Immanuel Kant, *Critique of Pure Reason*

Socrates annoyed the professional educators of his day—the sophists—with his persistent questions about their enterprise. "Just what exactly is it that you do?" he wanted to know. A conference held at Yale in April 1998 asked seven prominent philosophers to turn this Socratic question back on themselves. Before an audience consisting mostly of philosophy professors and graduate students, they asked "What is philosophy? What exactly are we philosophy professors doing, and what *should* we do?" The present volume is a collection of papers presented at the conference.[1] Although written for an audience of scholars, the articles are accessible to undergraduates and educated non-philosophers.

In his reflections on the nature of philosophy, Martin Heidegger remarked that "the question about the nature of something awakens at those times when the thing whose nature is being questioned has become obscure and confused, when at the same time the relationship of men to what is being questioned has become uncertain or has even been shattered."[2] We seem to live in such a time, for contemporary philosophers share no unified conception of what philosophy has been or should become. The role of philosophy within the larger culture is somewhat ambiguous. From the European perspective, Karl-Otto Apel (Chapter 6) perceives there to be a boom of public interest in philosophy.[3] Nicholas Rescher, speaking to "the state of North American philosophy" in 1992, remarked that it "makes virtually no impact on the wider culture" although its place in our higher education system is secure and philosophical activity is flourishing.[4]

While there is little agreement about what philosophy is in theory, there is a very high degree of practical uniformity: in day-to-day life, most philosophers practice an academic trade that flourishes in the university. The dominant view within the profession seems to be that a 'genuine' philosopher—as opposed to a mere teacher of philosophy—is "a professor of philosophy who also publishes in his field."[5] This conception of philosophy as a sort of industrial production has spawned a gigantic increase in the number of books and journal articles dedicated to philosophical questions. But despite the generally high quality and technical sophistication of their publications, today's industrialized philosophers risk selling their birthright—the Socratic spirit—for professional status and prestige. The problem is not merely that professional legitimacy is conferred only upon those who have mastered a certain technical apparatus. For in addition, the present journeyman tactics in philosophy often render it, as Barry Stroud laments, "sterile, empty, and boring" (Chapter 1).

But most important, as Stroud also notes, this "professionalized scientistic conception" of philosophy is "not sufficiently philo-

C. P. Ragland and Sarah Heidt

sophical" because "it is compatible at a certain point with the absence of philosophy." According to Stroud, this professionalization has resulted in "complacency" at best, and at worst "blindness" to what is philosophically important. Philosophy, as Allen Wood points out, "is a *self-reflective* activity" (Chapter 4), and hence cannot take its own nature for granted without losing itself. Stroud suggests that philosophers might free their discipline from a certain amount of self-imposed shallowness if they stop taking the nature of their enterprise for granted. He calls for serious grappling with the question "What is philosophy?"

But why suppose that philosophers *need* to inquire into the nature of philosophy any more than artists need to ponder the nature of art?[6] The greatness of painters is measured by the quality of their works, not by their musings in art theory. Similarly, it does not seem that philosophers need to delve into the nature of philosophy in order to do *their* work well. As Allen Wood says, "philosophical reflection gains its importance more from what it discovers about the objects of its reflection (about the nature of knowledge, goodness, beauty, and so forth) than from its own nature simply as philosophical reflection."

The nature of philosophy is not a preeminent philosophical question, and philosophers can be great without writing essays on meta-philosophy. Philosophy would rapidly cease to be interesting if it turned from other questions to an obsession with its own nature, and doubtless many great philosophers have never written about what philosophy is. Wood is right that the value of philosophy lies in the light it throws on what is not philosophy. Stroud himself says that "there always has to be something more to reflect on, or to start from, than just the activity of philosophizing itself. There has to be something we think, something we are trying to understand, some puzzling phenomenon or aspect of the world. . . . There must be something we are involved in that is not philosophy."

Nevertheless, the question "What is philosophy?" does seem to be a necessary part of philosophy. All the contributors to this book seem to agree that philosophy is—or aims at—relentless, comprehensive examination and criticism of concepts and inferences. But as Stroud suggests, philosophy would fail to be fully relentless and comprehensive if it examined and criticized the foundational concepts of other disciplines without raising questions about its own core concepts—about what makes a theory "philosophical," what it means to "accept" such a theory, and so forth. The philosophical charge to "know thyself" applies just as much to us *qua* philosophers as it does to us *qua* human beings (even if the latter sort of self-knowledge is vastly more important than the former).

Excessive professionalization is more than just a threat to the self-reflectiveness of academic philosophy. It appears as a symptom of the much-heralded "end of philosophy." In the ruthless division of labor characteristic of academic professionalization, the traditional goal of philosophy—the production of an articulated and integrated vision of humanity and its place in the universe—seems to have gone missing.[7]

But perhaps this is no real loss. Perhaps it is actually good that philosophers are no longer trying to construct grand metaphysical systems. Some of the contributors to this book are committed to problematizing the notion of an absolute standpoint or conception of reality. Stroud, for example, thinks that we can never achieve a detached theoretical point of view on the world, and that although such a viewpoint would perhaps be what philosophy aspires to, the only understanding we can actually attain is a human, self-understanding. There is no "view from nowhere." One could argue that philosophical diversity is actually a sign of progress; grand strategies are doomed either to fail or to point us in dangerous directions.

But is the abandonment of a totalizing vision tantamount to the end of philosophy? "In the contemporary end of philosophy," said Emmanuel Levinas, "philosophy has found a new lease on life."[8] Nicholas Rescher notes that "there is more academic hay to be made nowadays by debunking metaphysics and epistemology as traditionally conceived than by practicing them."[9] Although the philosophers in this book exhibit a wide range of concern over the so-called death of philosophy, they express a clear interest in the future of philosophy. Despite their differences, the chapters in this volume represent overwhelming continuity with the tradition and an optimistic response to "fin de siècle disillusionment" with the philosophical enterprise.

There are as many answers to the question "What is philosophy?" as there are philosophers. This is at least in part because the disarmingly short question contains, or gives rise to, many other questions. It is therefore difficult to keep the question manageable. Each of the philosophers in this volume seeks to define this daunting question more exactly, and each arrives at a unique interpretation of the question. Nevertheless, all the contributors share three important points of similarity.

First, they seem to agree that the question "What is philosophy?" demands an account of how philosophy differs from other academic disciplines and social practices. When we ask what philosophy is, we also ask what it is not; we seek to demarcate it from non-philosophy. We can say, without much controversy, that philosophy aims at some kind of very general understanding of the world. For example, Stroud says that philosophy is "reflection on very general aspects of the world, and especially those aspects that involve or impinge on the lives of human beings." This echoes Sellars's claim that philosophers aim to see "how things, in the largest sense of the term, hang together, in the largest sense of the term."[10] But this characterization of philosophy seems too vague; as Stroud notes, "Every culture has thoughts and attitudes about fundamental features of a human being's relation to the rest of the universe, about death and human finitude, and about the appropriate ways of interacting with other human beings. Those are the kinds of things philosophy is about. But not every way of coming to terms with them, even every way of thinking about them, amounts to philosophy." Any facile characterization of philosophy in terms of its very general subject matter fails to answer the question of demarcation. Most of us have the intuitive sense that philosophy, religion, art and science are all different despite the fact that they all aim (at least in part) to express how things "hang together" in an extremely general sense; we want any answer to the question "What is philosophy?" to account for that intuition. Though most of the chapters in this book address the question of demarcation, they answer it in very different ways.[11]

Second, the authors take "What is philosophy?" to be a largely normative question. The question has both descriptive and normative dimensions. When asked descriptively, the question means "What is philosophy *in fact?*"; when asked normatively, it means "What *ought* philosophy to be?"[12] Though most of the papers collected here do discuss facts about philosophy in some way (Harries and Apel, especially, examine the present state of the discipline), by and large the focus is on the normative question.[13] This preoccupation with normativity betrays something important: while philosophy may need to take facts into account, it seems to focus primarily on (broadly) normative claims about either what we ought to think or what we ought to do. By addressing the normative question many of the authors seem to agree that "the topic of philosophy is normativity in all its guises."[14]

Finally, all the contributors here agree that philosophy is not simply reducible to a set of problems, a body of doctrine, or a series of conclusions. As Stroud says, "Philosophy . . . is an activity, not a set of doctrines or truths at all. Nor is its point or goal to discover philosophical theses or doctrines." For Stroud, philosophy is a way of questioning that can never come to rest in an established theory, because it "depends on undying curiosity, and the pursuit of limitless enquiry." Not all the contributors would follow Stroud to this ultimate conclusion. Some think that even if philosophy ends where belief in theses and doctrines begins, philosophy at least *aims* to establish such claims ("philosophical theses" are the end of philosophy as both its termination and its *telos*). Others even appear to think that philosophy includes not only the search for, but also the belief in, certain kinds of theses. Nevertheless, all the contributors seem to agree with Stroud that we cannot *define* philosophy by the theses it establishes. Even if there were a "philosophical catechism," a complete list of philosophical questions and answers, no one could learn what philosophy is by reading it. For the distinctiveness of philosophy lies not in the answers it produces or the questions it asks, but in the unique *way* it asks those questions. Despite their disagreements about whether philosophy produces or even aims at answers, the contributors to this volume agree that philosophy is a process and not a product. Before treating the question "What is philosophy?" either descriptively or normatively, they all ineluctably transform this static question, conceiving the essence of philosophy dynamically by focusing on the very activity of philosophy: What is it to philosophize? By approaching philosophy as an activity rather than a product, the contributors must consider not only the act but also the agent and the aim. Who is the philosopher and what is he or she hoping to accomplish? But further, to what or to whom is the philosopher obligated? Why philosophize?

The philosophers in this book return to the basic questions that animated Plato and Aristotle. In the *Nichomachean Ethics*, Aristotle said that true arguments are most useful not only for knowledge, but also for life, because "they stimulate those who understand them to live according to them."[15] Was Aristotle correct?

Is philosophy a purely theoretical activity, or does it have practical application? Is it a self-contained intellectual pursuit, or does it spill over into the way we live our lives outside the study? Wood claims that philosophy is the attempt of unaided reason not only to understand the world, but to act in it. If this is so, we ought to consider how the abandonment of a totalizing vision affects the social function of philosophy. Does the increasing technicality and fragmentation of the discipline lead philosophers to think of themselves as isolated intellectual laborers, and of philosophy as a purely theoretical undertaking? Or will philosophers in the twenty-first century be in a position to make a unique contribution toward social change?

Certainly the general public—even the general "intellectual" public—has failed to appreciate many of the intense and powerful developments in philosophy during the latter half of the twentieth century. The abstractness or difficulty of contemporary philosophy may be partially responsible, but philosophers have also blamed the professionalization of philosophy in the positivist period. Tyler Burge points out that the lines of communication between philosophy and the rest of the culture have become "lamentably weak" and "positivism's harsh judgement of the cognitive value of most of non-scientific culture should probably be given much of the blame."[16] Burge's remark illuminates the connection that Stroud and others see between the scientific pretensions and the sterile professionalization of philosophy in our time. Organizers of the recent World Congress of Philosophy expressed concern that philosophical fields have become so specialized that philosophy itself is becoming an increasingly irrelevant academic sub-specialty. In this book, Martha Nussbaum is particularly critical of philosophers who are unable or unwilling to overcome their professional habits and vocabularies in order to reach out effectively to readers beyond their discipline.

Nussbaum's contribution, Public Philosophy and International

Feminism (Chapter 5), expresses her commitment to making a difference in the world. Philosophy, on her view, has something vital to contribute to the guidance of public life and should play a role in international political debates. Nussbaum says that philosophers are called to many things beyond Socratic questioning: they must critically examine economic models and arguments, enter debates about medical ethics, analyze foundational concepts in the social sciences, and construct theories. Philosophers, she argues, are particularly well-suited to these kinds of subtle, rigorous, and critical conceptual work. Philosophical inquiries into such foundational concepts are, Nussbaum avers, "sometimes viewed as examples of obsessive intellectual fussiness; they have, however, important practical consequences, which need to be taken into account in practical political programs."

What, then, are the practical implications of the conceptual explication Nussbaum calls for? Her own work has tried to show economists that their models make substantive philosophical commitments that need to be scrutinized. She and Nobel Prize–winning economist Amartya Sen have tried to get philosophers and economists to discuss together the foundational concepts of development economics—in particular, the concept of "the quality of life." Nussbaum suggests that the conceptions of well-being currently dominant in economics, conceptions which suggest that well-being correlates strongly with GNP per capita or with desire satisfaction, are too simplistic; they would tell policy makers that women in developing countries are "well off" even when they still face serious forms of oppression and abuse. These abuses are invisible to economists operating with a crude conception of well-being. Through explicating this conception and exposing it to rational criticism, Nussbaum and Sen hope to establish the superiority of a "capabilities approach" to well-being, according to which "quality of life should be measured not in terms of satisfactions or even the distribution of resources, but in terms of what people are actually able to do and to be, in certain central areas of human functioning."

By exposing the inadequacy of current conceptions of well-being and developing a better alternative, philosophy can actually help ameliorate the lives of poor women in developing countries, provided that economists and policy makers are willing to listen to the philosophers, and the philosophers are willing to express their ideas in a clear and readable fashion. Nussbaum sees her project as one example of how philosophical concern with "highly abstract ideas about the nature of anger, the social origins of greed, and so on," can give public policy making "a critical apparatus it did not have before, names of abuses that were not named before, and so forth." Philosophy, she argues, can provide foundational and systematic understanding to guide prescriptions and laws.

Others, however, suggest that we should beware the idea of "professional expertise" that philosophers might claim to have with regard to practical questions. Such worries were present at philosophy's inception—we find them expressed in Socrates' protestations of ignorance and in his criticism of the Sophists who claimed "expert" status with regard to ethical, political, and other practical matters. Today, Richard Rorty is an exemplary opponent of the notion that philosophers are experts on all actual and possible "language games." Rorty has also said that he doesn't see philosophy as criticizing anything: "We do not need philosophy for social criticism: we have economics, sociology, the novel, psychoanalysis, and many other ways to criticize society."[17] In general, he would have us realize "how little theoretical reflection is likely to help us with our current problems."[18]

In contrast to Wood and Nussbaum, Stroud argues that philosophy neither has practical consequences, nor aims at them. According to Stroud, philosophy "is not a matter of arriving at conclusions

C. P. Ragland and Sarah Heidt

that are applied or used to guide or order one's life. Philosophy is thought, or reflection, that is done purely for the sake of understanding something, solely to find out what is so with respect to those aspects of the world that puzzle us." We pursue philosophy not as means to a better (individual or collective) life, but simply because it is inherently valuable activity. Philosophy does not enjoy the patronage of the university and society "for any of the specific conclusions it is expected to reach. It is regarded as more important that the activity should go on then that it should have this or that specified outcome. Results, in the form of conclusions reached, or propositions established, are not what matters."

Harries (Chapter 2) seems to fall somewhere between Stroud and the practically oriented philosophers on this point. On the one hand, he endorses Aristotle's claim that philosophers seek knowledge "not because [it] might prove useful or help them find the right way," but because "it is its own reward." "Without such autotelic activities," Harries continues, "life would be empty." On the other hand, there are points at which Harries seems to agree with Wood that philosophy aims for right action, or at least for an *ethos*— a way of existing in the world. Echoing Wittgenstein, Harries says that philosophy begins when we lose our way, when we no longer feel secure about our place in the world and our way of life, when we do not know what to do. Born of this anxiety, philosophy asks "What is the right way?" In some cases at least, we start doing philosophy for the sake of knowing how to live.

Harries's remarks suggest an inclusive picture of how philosophy relates to practical action. If we presume that philosophy must *either* aim at action *or not*, we create a false dichotomy. Some philosophical inquiry aims at rational action, and some at understanding for its own sake. Neither practically oriented nor purely theoretical philosophy has an exclusive claim to be the "real thing."

Philosophical questions can gain significance *either* from their relation to "projects that are part of life," *or* from the intrinsic worth of the "escape from ignorance" and the knowledge of truth.

But even if Harries admits that some philosophy is done for the sake of rational action, he does not agree with Wood that philosophy includes such action. Wood claims that philosophy is the attempt of reason to act in the world: "Reason is a capacity to know the world, but chiefly it is a capacity to act in it, and since reason is also oriented toward society, its vocation above all is to transform the social order, actualizing the Enlightenment ideals of liberty, equality and fraternity." Harries, by contrast, thinks that perpetual questioning is essential to philosophy. "Philosophy remains alive only as long as the question: what is the right way? continues to be asked because that way remains questionable, because our place and vocation remains uncertain. Were philosophy to determine or decide on the right way . . . it would have done its work and come to an end. This is why the birth of a science has meant so often the death of a part of philosophy. Science is defined at least in part by a determination of what constitutes the right way or proper method. A scientist who calls that way into question returns to the philosophical origin of science." Such questioning must be suspended when we act; action, like scientific progress, requires us to take some practical maxims as established guides rather than as objects of critical scrutiny. Therefore, because the essence of philosophy is critical scrutiny, philosophy itself cannot include the transformation of society, even if it is undertaken for the sake of such transformation.

If we suppose that some philosophy aims at rational action, while some pursues understanding for its own sake, it is natural to ask what unifies these two approaches to philosophy. What do they have in common? Why are both *philosophy?* Because both aim at self-understanding; both try to explicate foundational concepts and subject them to criticism—whether or not the resulting understanding is supposed to issue in action or social transformation. We are philosophers not because we ask the right *kind* (practical or impractical) of questions, but because we ask those questions in the right *sort of way*. From its beginning, as Nussbaum says, philosophy "has been that irritating gadfly that keeps asking questions about the core concepts—both its own and (irritatingly, but valuably) those of other disciplines and people." Regardless of their ultimate goals, philosophers probe foundational concepts to increase clarity; they have, in Nussbaum's words, "a commitment to the critical scrutiny of arguments that makes them good at refining distinctions, detecting fallacies," and understanding both sides in a dispute.

As Wood notes, the *philosophes* of the French Enlightenment also conceived of philosophy as the pursuit of self-knowledge. Wood makes the Enlightenment picture clear in his commentary on a passage of Dumarsais: "Rational or free action involves no exemption from having one's actions caused, and no absence of passion. It does not even involve any exemption from the universal human condition of walking in darkness. Through the darkness, however, philosophers walk with a torch of self-knowledge. By becoming aware of the causes that move them, they acquire the critical capacity of selecting which causes (which thoughts, conditions, sentiments, and passions) these will be. Philosophers, therefore, accept no principle at face value but seek the *origins* of their principles, so that they may take every maxim from its source, knowing thereby both its true worth and the limits of its applicability." The philosopher's primary task is to become aware of her own mind: to bring to light what is hidden, to make explicit what was before only implicit. But the purpose is not merely descriptive; the philosopher also seeks to *evaluate* what she brings to light. As Robert Brandom (Chapter 3) says:

I see the point of explicating concepts to be opening them up to rational *criticism*. The rational enterprise, the practice of giving and asking for reasons that lies at the heart of discursive activity, requires not only criticizing *beliefs* as false or unwarranted, but also criticizing *concepts*. Defective concepts distort our thought and constrain us by limiting the propositions and plans we can entertain as candidates for endorsement in belief and intention. This constraint operates behind our backs, out of our sight, since it limits what we are so much as capable of being aware of. Philosophy, in developing and applying tools for the rational criticism of concepts, seeks to free us from these fetters, by bringing the distorting influences out into the light of conscious day, exposing the commitments implicit in our concepts as vulnerable to rational challenge and debate.

Of all the contributors, Brandom presents most clearly this picture of philosophy as conceptual explication and evaluation. And though some of the contributors to this book are not friends of the Enlightenment, most seem to agree with Brandom's characterization of philosophy. Philosophy unpacks and evaluates notions that other disciplines take for granted.

When we engage in philosophical questioning, we throw ourselves into uncertainty about fundamental beliefs and concepts (even if, as human beings, we remain deeply committed to those beliefs and concepts). Insofar as it involves refusing to take things for granted, philosophy is an exercise in rational autonomy. Wood, Brandom, and Harries all emphasize that philosophy requires that we leave "the comfort and security of tutelage" and embrace the "risks and responsibilities of thinking for oneself."[19] Following Heidegger, Harries recasts Kantian autonomy in the language of au-

C. P. Ragland and Sarah Heidt

thenticity: "Philosophy, as I understand it, has its origin in a sense of homelessness that is intimately linked to the demand for authenticity, the demand that the individual should act and think for himself or herself." Those who pursue authentic thought cannot content themselves with "what has come to be established, accepted, and taken for granted." By demanding autonomy, philosophy questions the authority of history and nature, and "puts into question also the authority of philosophy."

Even Nussbaum opposes underwriting one's position by the mere appeal to philosophical authority. She complains that certain postmodernist relativists proceed without offering arguments by merely invoking the names of Foucault or Derrida. Her practical interests thus stem not only from her general conception of the philosopher as a "lawyer for unhappy humanity" but from her "universalist" approach. In a recent book, she defends a universal account of women's quality of life.[20] This practical engagement seems to be built upon a theoretical foundation that has more in common with the transcendental-pragmatic approach of Karl-Otto Apel than with any of the other approaches in the present volume.

Apel is the only representative herein of the "transcendental" mode of philosophizing. Generally speaking, a transcendental argument seeks to show that one thing is a non-causal condition on the possibility of another thing. Apel's brand of "discourse ethics," which seeks consensus through discussion, is at the same time a reflection on the presuppositions of argumentation. Apel divides philosophy into first philosophy and speculative metaphysics. First philosophy is sharply distinct from the sciences because "in its kernel, [it] does not contain any fallible hypotheses, but only the indisputable conditions of fallible hypotheses." Speculative metaphysics, on the other hand, lies "between first philosophy and the empirical sciences, providing the latter with seminal ideas for new paradigms of research, as philosophy in fact has done since the time of the pre-Socratics." He argues, along with Nussbaum, that an ethic of global justice requires us to have knowledge of ecological, social, and economic facts (although Nussbaum goes further and argues that philosophy must be informed by actual experience as well).

Even abstemious philosophers such as Stroud and Harries can agree that philosophers need to know a great deal about the world as it is revealed by other disciplines. For example, Stroud argues that although there are no facts *in* philosophy there must still be facts *for* philosophy: "There must be some 'data' . . . to reflect on" even if these facts are only convictions or attitudes. Harries also holds that "reality gives itself first of all as always already charged with meaning." Apel claims that even in a multicultural society that respects differences, we can and should agree on some universal norms. Similarly, Nussbaum works to provide a philosophical backing for universalism that can be taken into account by those who are responsible for developing practical programs.

Allen Wood's Enlightenment ideals also speak to the task of forging a global culture that is genuinely universal. Earlier we claimed that to ask about the activity of philosophizing is also to ask: Who is a philosopher? Wood focuses on this most explicitly, reminding us that for Kant, to call oneself a philosopher showed no small degree of self-conceit. Just as philosophy itself, as a completed science of wisdom, does not yet exist, the philosopher too must remain an ideal figure. Having disputed any special status for the philosopher, and indeed denying that philosophers should even be in the business of making "universal validity claims," Rorty would turn philosophical discourse into persuasive and edifying conversation. Harries sees this pragmatic view of philosophy as of a piece with its institutionalization: it becomes merely an "intellectual technology"—the philosophy industry collecting various discourses for its "toolbox." According to Apel, Rorty's conversationalist pragmatism forecloses any sort of criticism that might be made against it and thus marks the end of philosophy by allowing for no context-independent validity claims.

Like Rorty, Stroud is suspicious of Apel's attempt to discover transcendental or necessary conditions of any possible human thought or discourse. Stroud thinks that no transcendental perspective or absolute point of view is possible for us. But he rejects the extreme view which holds that there are no facts or truths of any kind, only agreement or consensus. Nevertheless, he might appear to go a step further than Rorty by denying even that the primary purpose of philosophical writing is persuasion. Stroud transforms the question "What is philosophy?" into the question "How do I see philosophy?" In so doing, he exemplifies his view that the activity of philosophy has to do with making things clear to oneself. He offers a definition of philosophy that states a clear telos: "Philosophy is thought, or reflection, that is done purely for the sake of understanding something." But the end product of such understanding is not (or should not be) a philosophical thesis or theory. Stroud finds that contemporary philosophers are often "insufficiently critical of what a philosophical thesis or theory amounts to, and what it means to adopt or accept such a thing. That makes philosophical theorizing look too much like accepting an ideology or a creed or a religion. It does not take into philosophical consideration the very attitude of so-called acceptance itself, or the very status of the doctrines or theory accepted."

Both Rorty and Stroud represent the strain of postanalytic philosophy which holds that we should try to "get out from under" certain basic questions of philosophy, rather than trying to answer them. Following Wittgenstein, the idea is that the only philosophical work left to be done is to dissolve traditional metaphysical problems by diagnosing them as pseudo-problems. Stroud rejects the label *therapeutic* for what he is recommending, preferring instead the term *diagnostic*. Wittgenstein also held that philosophy "requires a resignation . . . of feeling and not of intellect."[21] But because such resignation is so difficult to achieve, and because the desire to gain an objective, neutral perspective on ourselves is so great, Stroud thinks that philosophers will always have to cope with certain sorts of problems. Stroud, then, is not worried about the end of philosophy. Against Stroud's "diagnostic" view, Apel argues that philosophy should not confuse self-criticism with "fashionable generalisations of mere feelings of resignation" that "erupt in pseudo-metaphysical statements concerning the finiteness and complete fallibility of our capacities of reason."

Apel also identifies Jean-François Lyotard, Michel Foucault, and Jacques Derrida as philosophers of the end of philosophy. Because Apel thinks that anyone who engages in philosophical argument presupposes certain validity claims, both postanalytic skeptics in Anglophone philosophy and postmodern continental philosophers are engaging in what Apel calls "performative self-contradiction." A philosopher must be self-critical and self-reflexive but he or she must not be self-contradictory. For Apel, then, one of the distinctive ways in which philosophy can end is by dissolving into a decadent postmodern rhetorical genre.

Karsten Harries is also concerned with this way in which philosophy might end, but it is clearly not his main concern. Harries thinks that the more problematic form of the death of philosophy—its marginalization—occurs bit by bit when the questions of deepest concern to a society are taken to be asked and answered by other disciplines. This sentiment is echoed by Stroud, who explains the lack of "results" in philosophy as follows: "as soon as there are real results, it no longer counts as philosophy." Science has progressed by securing its proper method; this, Harries says, has resulted in its

C. P. Ragland and Sarah Heidt

"emancipation from the tutelage of philosophy." The success of the natural sciences is disquieting for philosophers, because it seems to leave little for philosophy to contribute.

Harries claims that "science presents philosophy today with what I take to be its most pressing problem." Science aims at objectivity, at an understanding of the world that is free from the distortions of individual, cultural, and social perspectives. The danger of postmodern philosophy, according to Harries, is that it would have us believe that science is "just another story." It thus fails to take up the real task of confronting science. The success of science, he thinks, casts a shadow over our everyday lives because science can in principle make no room for freedom or for personhood; "the scientist's pursuit of truth . . . has lead to a reduction of reality to a collection of mute facts, raw material that lacks meaning until appropriated and put to use by human subjects," and this view of reality "does violence to our experience of both persons and things."

The task that now lies ahead for philosophers is to recognize the legitimacy and the validity of science in order to circumscribe its limits. Perhaps philosophy departments should give more weight to the philosophy and history of science. But even this is a problematic answer. As Wilfrid Sellars explained in his landmark *Empiricism and the Philosophy of Mind:*

> As long as there was no such subject as 'philosophy of science', all students of philosophy felt obligated to keep at least one eye part of the time on both the methodological and the substantive aspects of the scientific enterprise. And if the result was often a confusion of the task of philosophy with the task of science, and almost equally often a projection of the framework of the latest scientific speculations into the common sense picture of the world . . . at least it had the merit of ensuring that reflection on the nature and

implications of scientific discourse was an integral and vital part of philosophical thinking generally. But now that philosophy of science has nominal as well as real existence, there has arisen the temptation to leave it to the specialists, and to confuse the sound idea that philosophy is not science with the mistaken idea that philosophy is independent of science.[22]

What, then, *is* the relationship of philosophy to science? Possible answers to this question fall along a continuum. Despite his awareness that philosophy is a distinctively self-reflexive enterprise in a way that physics is not, Wood claims that science and philosophy are "not fundamentally different." The sciences are simply parts of philosophy. Harries also claims that at the origin of science lies philosophy, but he takes this to imply that the two modes of inquiry are of a fundamentally different order. He is closer in this regard to Stroud, who sees philosophy as a different sort of enterprise from science altogether. Whereas physics or chemistry includes a basic core of knowledge that any physicist or chemist (of a certain time and place) accepts, philosophers share no such accepted body of doctrine. For Stroud, even recourse to tradition as a source of problems is of no help in this regard, whereas Robert Brandom's version of Hegelianism sees rationality itself as imposing an obligation to "construe histories as revelatory of natures." The very form of reason consists in rewriting history to make things intelligible. Philosophy has a history, and in attempting to understand that history we make ourselves as discursive beings the topic of philosophical inquiry. Brandom thinks that our particular goal is to understand the discursive as such—in Sellars's phrase, "the game of giving and asking for reasons."[23] And this goal of *understanding* is distinct from science's goal of *knowledge*.

While other disciplines try to understand some particular topic or other, philosophy seeks to understand understanding in general, which is for Brandom a normative notion. Philosophy's concern with normativity clearly sets it apart from the descriptive concerns of the natural and social sciences, and its preoccupation with conceptual norms distinguishes it from the arts and other humanistic disciplines. The questions of philosophy are thus not like questions in the natural sciences because their topic—conceptual and discursive activity—is cultural. Even so, Brandom suggests, such activity should not be studied in the way that the social sciences study cultural objects, because the aim of the philosopher is expressive. The social sciences would explain the unfolding of concepts by showing why they arise at one time rather than at another time, whereas the philosopher tries to unpack explicitly what the content of a concept is through the intricate tracing of inferential connections. Brandom's conceptual clarification viewed as historically sensitive rational reconstruction is thus somewhat different from Nussbaum's notion of conceptual analysis. Despite the distance that separates them with regard to philosophy's practical role, Brandom and Wood thus share a fairly traditional outlook in which philosophy is seen as addressing the nature and conditions of our rationality. Both see the normative realm, the realm of reason, as the realm of freedom. This simply underscores, for Harries, the fact that the philosopher does not tell us "what is the case." We turn to science for that. But science knows nothing of what ought to be—and its reduction of reality to mere facts leaves no room for free persons. Wood sees philosophy as the way for humanity to reach maturity, for people to take responsibility for their thoughts and actions. Harries is in agreement with this conception of the philosophical enterprise. He sees the pursuit of truth for truth's sake as an exercise of freedom. But this freedom is primarily a self-transcendence or "leave-taking" from the everyday world, rather than a descent into the cave in order to rescue those still bound.

The notion of a philosophical rescue team neglects the fact that the freedom of the philosophers themselves remains bound and their understanding only partial. The chapters in this book highlight a kind of practical paradox that is essential to philosophy. Philosophy, in principle at least, aims to explicate and rationally criticize all fundamental beliefs and concepts, but such a project cannot get off the ground unless we are willing to accept some concepts and beliefs uncritically. We noted earlier that for Harries, philosophy cannot spill over into action because action must follow practical maxims that remain free from critical scrutiny. But rational criticism is itself a kind of action, and so must begin by taking at least some maxims for granted. Philosophy may pierce the darkness, but the interior of its torch must remain hidden from the light; it may aim to free us from tradition, but it does so only by inculcating in us the Socratic tradition. For this reason, as Wood says, philosophy "can never be what it aims to be." Philosophy strives for a complete transparency that must forever elude us. Socrates was right when in the *Symposium* he said that philosophy is not something at rest, but something caught between two irreconcilable realms, a perpetual striving that draws its life from tension.[24]

Notes

1. This volume contains all the papers presented at the conference except the one by Richard Rorty.

2. Martin Heidegger, *What Is Philosophy?*, trans. William Kluback and Jean T. Wilde (Albany: NCUP, 1956), 43.

3. Parenthetical references in the text are to chapters of the present volume.

4. Nicholas Rescher, "American Philosophy Today," *Review of Metaphysics* 46 (4), 734.

5. Karsten Harries (Chapter 2).

C. P. Ragland and Sarah Heidt

6. The analogy between these two questions is suggested by Harries (Chapter 2), Wood (Chapter 4), and Stroud (Chapter 1).

7. This characterization of the traditional goal of philosophy comes from Wilfrid Sellars, *Empiricism and the Philosophy of Mind* (Cambridge: Harvard University Press, 1997), 81.

8. Emmanuel Levinas, *Face to Face with Levinas,* ed. Richard A. Cohen (Albany: State University of New York Press, 1986), 33.

9. Rescher, "American Philosophy Today," 737.

10. Wilfrid Sellars, "Philosophy and the Scientific Image of Man," in *Frontiers of Science and Philosophy,* ed. Robert Colodny (Pittsburgh: University of Pittsburgh Press, 1962), 37.

11. Indeed, at the Yale conference, Rorty seemed to think that demarcating philosophy from other disciplines is the most interesting task engendered by the question "What is philosophy?" He reformulated that question for himself by asking what, over the past century, has distinguished the philosophers from other Western intellectuals.

12. Compare Wood's distinction between analytical and apologetic versions of the question (Chapter 4).

13. For example, Wood says he will "try to say what I think philosophy has been (albeit imperfectly) that it most of all *should* go on being" [emphasis added], and Apel tries to answer for himself "what I think [philosophy] *should* be today" [emphasis added]. Nussbaum says that philosophers are good at the kind of critical reflection that "all thinkers about society—and indeed, at some level all citizens—*should* be doing, but often don't" [emphasis added], thereby implicitly defining philosophy in terms of a norm or ideal of critical reflection.

14. Robert Brandom (Chapter 3).

15. Aristotle, *Nicomachean Ethics* X:1, 1172b, 4–7.

16. Tyler Burge, "Philosophy of Language and Mind: 1950–1990," *Philosophical Review* 101 (1), 3.

17. Richard Rorty, "After Philosophy, Democracy," in *The American Philosopher,* ed. Giovanna Borradori (Chicago: University of Chicago Press, 1994), 117.

18. Richard Rorty, "Philosophy as Science, Metaphor, Politics," in

Essays on Heidegger and Others: Philosophical Papers Volume 2 (New York: Cambridge University Press, 1992), 25.

19. The quotation is from Wood (Chapter 4).

20. Martha Nussbaum, *Women and Human Development: The Capabilities Approach* (Cambridge: Cambridge University Press, 2000).

21. Ludwig Wittgenstein, *Philosophical Occasions 1912–1951* (Indianapolis: Hackett, 1993), 161.

22. Sellars, *Empiricism and the Philosophy of Mind*, 79–80.

23. Robert Brandom, "Study Guide," in Sellars, *Empiricism and the Philosophy of Mind*, 123.

24. Plato, *Symposium*, 201d–204c.

C. P. Ragland and Sarah Heidt

1
What Is Philosophy?

Barry Stroud

Faced, as I now am, with the question "What is philosophy?," my first reaction is that the question is absurd. On a little reflection I find that it is not so much the question that is absurd as the attempt to answer it. Then, getting more personal, I realize that what is even more absurd is for *me* to try to answer it. But now, having reached this more personal perspective, I can shift the question a little, so it becomes not "What is philosophy?" but only "How do I see philosophy?" That is still daunting—how *do* I see philosophy?—but it feels more manageable. But then any answer I might give is not likely to be of wide interest. It will be like the message of a flea, working away at his own square inch of flesh, reporting on "How I see the elephant." Trying to answer the large, impersonal question is absurd or discouraging in the way that it is absurd or discouraging to try to answer questions like "What is painting?" or "What is music?" It is not that nothing can be said, even something that is true. But what can be said that would be helpful to someone who wants an answer?

For one thing, painting and music and philosophy are human

activities with a history. They are as they are here and now because of the ways they were elsewhere and in earlier times. A large part of understanding them lies in understanding how they got to be the way they are from what they were before. But the completely general questions seem to ask simply "What are they?" And someone who asks that question out of complete ignorance—someone from Mars, say—is not likely to be satisfied with a story of how one kind of painting or music or philosophy led to another, and eventually to what we have here and now.

This brings out part of the absurdity in trying to answer the completely general question: it is left indeterminate what someone who asks the question wants to know. How much is such a person supposed to know already, or not to know, about human life? Where are we allowed to start in trying to tell someone what painting or music or philosophy is? Someone from Mars, say, who has never visited this planet, might be satisfied with being told that here on earth some of us paint, and that painting is marking a surface with color, or that we enjoy music, which is sound and silence ordered by a composer in certain ways. That is true, as far as it goes, but it is probably not going to satisfy anyone a little closer to home who asks what painting, or music, is. And the same is true of "What is philosophy?" or even of my more personal question: "How do you see philosophy?"

Another part of the absurdity in trying to answer the completely general question is that philosophy is many different things, and it has been conducted in many different ways. There is no reason to insist that it be only one thing, or that it can be summed up or defined in some illuminating way even for those who know a great deal about human life. That is why I restrict myself to saying how I see philosophy.

But there is another disclaimer to make even about that. I am suspicious of, and not very interested in, what painters say about their own paintings, for example. Technical details of execution are fine, materials and procedures fascinating, but when it comes to what the painting is really "about" or what the painter was really doing—not to mention what painting is in general—I don't think the painter is in any special position. The best thing to do is to look closely at the painting itself. That is what shows what it is and what it does, and what the painter was doing in painting it (if anything shows it). I have the same feeling about philosophy. It is much better—more reliable—to look at what a philosopher does in a particular case than to listen to what he or she says about what is being done. It is in the actual work that a philosopher's conception of philosophy, or his or her way of doing it, is really to be found. So I am suspicious of pronouncements, even by philosophers, about what philosophy is, or how it ought to be done. It is a real philosophical problem, I think, to say what is going on in a piece of philosophizing. The philosopher who is doing it is not necessarily in a privileged position about it.

With all these reservations in mind, I can nonetheless try to say something about what philosophy is—or how I see it. Just as it is true, but not very enlightening, to say that painting is marking a surface with color, so, at that same level of banal truth we can say that philosophy is thought. It is reflection on very general aspects of the world, and especially those aspects that involve or impinge on the lives of human beings. Human beings are those who carry out philosophical reflection, so it can be said to be a form of self-reflection. But not just any thought—even any self-reflective thought about very general aspects of the world that involve or impinge on the lives of human beings—is philosophy. Nor is all marking a surface with color painting, or all ordered combinations of sound and silence music.

This does not take us very far toward an answer to the question of what is special or unique about philosophy, but it does give us something. It points to something important, whatever the special or unique characteristics of philosophical thinking turn out to be. The important but not always acknowledged fact is that philosophy does not necessarily exist, and certainly does not thrive, in every society or culture. But every society or culture surely has some set of ideas about the way things are in general, and how they do and do not impinge on the lives of human beings. Some such general conception of the world, and some conception of themselves on the part of human beings, seems essential to, or at least universal in, all human life.

All human beings have certain interests and concerns, and certain fears and aspirations, which in one form or another are present in human life wherever it appears. And something institutional or social is needed for human beings to cope with or pursue those natural concerns, and to provide ways for groups of people to live together in some kind of unity. That is a large part of what a culture is, or does. But I do not regard the contents of all such cultural formations as philosophy, or each one of them as *a* philosophy. Every culture has thoughts and attitudes about fundamental features of a human being's relation to the rest of the universe, about death and human finitude, and about the appropriate ways of interacting with other human beings. Those are the kinds of things philosophy is about. But not every way of coming to terms with them, even every way of thinking about them, amounts to philosophy.

This is obvious in one way simply from the fact that there are a great many societies, in both the past and the present, for whom there are more important things than philosophy. Concerns about the life and death of human beings, about their relations to the world and to other human beings, must be attended to before the possibility, or even the conception, of philosophy could begin to arise. Philosophy exists, or flourishes, only under certain social conditions, not all. But if societies in even the most desperate circumstances, where there is no place for philosophy, nonetheless need certain shared understandings or ideas of themselves and their relation to the rest of the world in order to cohere and function at all, then the presence of such ideas does not necessarily amount to philosophy.

Obviously, a society must be pretty advanced, compared to the minimum conditions needed to function or even to flourish, in order for that society to support or make room for philosophy. Philosophy needs reasonably benign social conditions, and a relatively high level of economic development, at least for some of the people. But that alone is no guarantee that philosophy will have an official place in such a culture. Of course, philosophy can be done outside, or even against, an official culture. But that happens only where a tradition of previous philosophizing has not been completely extinguished. And even then it is difficult, and in the end does not lead to much in philosophical terms, except possibly keeping the tradition somehow available until more promising times.

Those repressive states that have attacked or tried to suppress philosophy by turning their unemployed and harassed philosophers into street sweepers or window washers do not lack a set of ideas which they expect their citizens to share and to guide their lives by. The doctrines they promulgate are general ideas and principles about the ends and value of human life and how best to achieve them. But they are not for that reason alone what I would regard as philosophy. They might even be *called* "philosophy," at least by the state that is trying to enforce them. But that doesn't mean that such states, or even their subjects who accept the ideas and live by them, are supporting or engaging in philosophy.

A society must be not only fairly advanced, but fairly comfortable with itself, to provide an official place for the best that philosophy can offer. By now, for us, it is hard to think of any place other than a university where that might be done—at least systematically and communally. That was not always so. The university has not been with us as long as philosophy has. But the age of royal or aristocratic patronage—or any form of private patronage—is behind us. Much work now being done in philosophy is supported by forms of social patronage other than the university. Resources that could obviously be put to pressing social uses sometimes go to philosophers. This is one mark of the advanced state, even the civility, of our Western culture. It is also perhaps a mark of our society's attitudes toward some of those pressing social issues. But the university now is the place where philosophy thrives.

This strikes me as both a good and a bad thing. It is bad because, as the university becomes increasingly professionalized, it has increasingly professionalized philosophy. This, in my opinion, has rendered much more of philosophy sterile, empty, and boring. What institutions demand from individuals, institutions get. And what universities, even the best universities, now demand from individual professors, on the whole, is quantity of publication, frequency of citation in the professional literature, widely certified distinction in the profession, and other quantifiable measures of an impressive resume. And that is what professors of philosophy are on the whole providing—to the detriment of philosophy as I see it.

But the connection between philosophy and the university is a good thing, too. It provides a place in which philosophy can be done, and with wise leadership can be done in conditions in which it can thrive. It requires teaching: the need to say clear things in public, and to make them accessible to others and subject to critical assessment. And teaching is what passes on the subject, or the tradition, if only in the form in which it is received by those now entering into it. The university also provides the freedom to think about something for a long time, and in new ways that might show no beneficial social effects. Philosophical work (even work that seems to go nowhere) is officially supported by the university, and so by the society at large, and not for any of the specific conclusions it is expected to reach. It is regarded as more important that the activity should go on than that it should have this or that specified outcome. Results, in the form of conclusions reached, or propositions established, are not what matters.

This is a good thing, as I see it, because I do not regard philosophy as a set of results or doctrines, in the sense of conclusions reached, or propositions established. It may well be that every society or culture needs ideas or beliefs or doctrines to give sense and direction to the lives of its members. And accepting a belief or doctrine, or espousing an ideology, is a form of thought, of thinking. But it is not the kind of thought that philosophy is. Or rather, that kind of thought is compatible with the absence of philosophy, or of what is valuable about philosophy at its best.

Religion, too, is a form of thinking, and is certainly about matters of great concern to human beings. But I think religious belief or religious thought is not the same as philosophy, or philosophical thought. As I put it a moment ago, it is compatible with the absence of philosophy, even though it includes beliefs, attitudes, and precepts that are based on general ideas about human beings and the world. Such thoughts and beliefs express a conception of the world, or a creed, but philosophy as I see it is not a creed. Nor is it the effort to discover or produce a creed.

I think the attitudes or motives out of which philosophy is pursued are not the same as a typically religious attitude or orientation. A philosopher is not fundamentally at peace with the world. He does not, as a philosopher, regard himself as somehow ultimately in good hands, and safe, and so willing to acquiesce in something that can or must be accepted without being understood. Of course, a philosopher, like everyone else, must acquiesce in the face of the facts—or at least of the facts that cannot be made otherwise. But philosophy depends on undying curiosity, and the pursuit of limitless enquiry. It arises out of a wish, or an attempt, to grasp the world as it is, as it is open to our view. The difficulty is to get the right, or the intellectually satisfying, view of it.

Philosophy is interesting and challenging to me personally only insofar as there is no other-worldly theological account of things. If I really thought there were, I believe I would not find serious thought about such matters interesting or rewarding in the way philosophy can be. The very effort would seem to founder on the epistemic difficulty of how far we could hope to penetrate the ultimately inscrutable ways of God or whatever else was thought to be in charge.

But even if I went in for such thoughts and beliefs, and they were important for the way I lived my life, I do not think that in accepting them I would be engaged in what I regard as philosophy. Not because philosophy as I think of it is idle and can have no effect on one's attitudes and one's relations to the world and to life. I mean only that philosophy as I understand it is different, and that it has its effects, if it does, in other ways. It is not a matter of arriving at conclusions that are applied to or used to guide or order one's life. Philosophy is thought, or reflection, that is done purely for the sake of understanding something, solely to find out what is so with respect to those aspects of the world that puzzle us. The activity is in a certain sense endless, even if it ends for each human being who engages in it. But that does not mean that it does not issue in anything, or that it has no effects. It is just that the effects, if they come, do not take the form of discoveries of conclusions or doctrines which serve to direct or guide one's life.

When I say that philosophy as I see it is not a creed, and not the search for a creed or set of doctrines—and so not a social or political creed or ideology, and not a religious creed or set of attitudes either—I also mean that it is not the search for what might be called a *philosophical* creed or a set of *philosophical* doctrines or theses either. Philosophy as I see it is an activity, not a set of doctrines or truths at all. Nor is its point or goal to discover philosophical theses or doctrines.

There is in that sense no such thing as, for example, twentieth-century philosophy or eighteenth-century philosophy, in the way there is such a thing as twentieth-century physics or present-day chemistry or molecular biology or seventeenth-century physics. Of course, there is lots of disagreement and uncertainty in those fields, and lots of activity leading off in different directions. And that has been true at every stage of their development. But there is such a thing as what all current physicists or chemists know: a body of doctrine that can be called truths of physics or chemistry as those subjects now stand. I don't mean that none of it will ever be changed, but only that there is a body of accepted truth that physicists or chemists share. It is the core, for now, of what physics, or chemistry, says: what is so, physically or chemically speaking. It is in that sense that I think there is no such thing as a body of philosophical doctrine, or truth: what is so, philosophically speaking. There is no such thing now, and there was no such thing in the past.

Many people will agree because, as they are happy to point out, philosophy makes no progress, and philosophers do not agree about anything—or at least not much. That is said to be because philosophers are inveterately, perhaps even inherently, disputatious, and because their problems are unreal, since there are no facts in philosophy, and no way to verify or falsify its claims. According to this idea, even when many philosophers do agree about something, that is all it is—widespread agreement, rather than the discovery of philosophical facts or truths.

In some circles now the view of philosophy I have just described is said to be true of all intellectual efforts to understand anything. There are held to be no facts or truths of any kind, even in physics or chemistry. There is just more widespread agreement in certain areas than in others, which leads us to speak of "facts" or "discoveries" in physics and chemistry and such fields, but not in politics or morals or philosophy. That usage itself is seen as just something else that most people agree about.

This more general view, if it can be called that, can perhaps make philosophy look not so bad after all, at least comparatively speaking. It turns out to differ from other intellectual pursuits only in the amount of agreement to be found in it. This could even make philosophers look good: maybe they are more courageous and more independently minded than those flocks of physicists and chemists and mathematicians who (on this view) are sheepishly going along with whatever consensus seems to be growing. But I will not dwell further on the sad story of this fashionable conception of human thought.

I think there is a different explanation for why there is no such thing as a body of doctrine, or a core of discovered truth, that represents the results of twentieth-century philosophy, or even eighteenth-century philosophy. I think it is because philosophy is just not the same kind of enterprise as physics or chemistry or other ways of coming to know about the world. It is true, of course, that certain *topics* or *questions* dominate philosophy in certain places and times, and certain ways of dealing with them prevail and then give way to other topics and methods. But those are interests and approaches and procedures, not results. They do not include a basic core which anyone doing philosophy at a certain time and place knows or accepts, and which represents philosophy's achievement up to that point.

There is of course a tradition of philosophical *works,* just as there is in painting and music. It is the works, and not something recognizable as their results, that constitute the tradition. That is why philosophy, like painting and music, must be understood at any given time at least in part historically. There is no way of understanding the issues and what is at stake other than seeing where they come from and why they present themselves at that time in the ways they do.

The need for a past, for a tradition to start from, is a commonplace of the history of painting. Painters paint as they do in response to the painting that precedes them. André Malraux dramatized the familiar point this way:

> It is a revealing fact that, when explaining how his vocation came to him, every great artist traces it back to the emotion he experienced at his contact with some specific work of art. . . . Never do we hear of someone who, out of the blue so to speak, feels a compulsion to "express" some scene or startling incident. . . . An old story goes that Cimabue was struck with admiration when he saw the shepherd-boy Giotto, sketching sheep. But, in the true biographies, it is never the sheep that inspire a Giotto with the love of painting; but, rather, his first sight of the paintings of a man like Cimabue. What makes the artist is that in his youth he was more deeply moved by his visual experience of works of art than by that of the things they represent.[1]

Something like this is no less true, I believe, of philosophy. G. E. Moore reports in his autobiography that he thinks "the main stimulus to philosophize" for him was "certain philosophical statements which [he] heard made in conversation." He says, "I do not think that the world or the sciences would ever have suggested to me any philosophical problems. What has suggested philosophical problems to me is things which other philosophers have said about the world or the sciences."[2] This is often cited as a defect or limitation of G. E. Moore and his philosophy, and indeed, sometimes, of so-called analytic or linguistic philosophy in general. It is thought to reveal the superficial and derivative, even parasitic, character of that philosophy, its dry academic or professorial sources, and its distance from the "real" problems that the world presents to any thoughtful, sensitive human being who is directly and passionately engaged with it. I think rather that the observation shows Moore's acuteness, and his honesty. Whatever one might think of Moore's limitations, perhaps even his blindnesses, as a philosopher, he was not blind or limited in this case. What he reports about himself is something I believe to be true of philosophy in general. I find it interesting that many philosophers would deny it, and would regard it as demeaning or indicative of shallowness to acknowledge that it is true of them.

Of course, those philosophers will concede that it is necessary to become acquainted with philosophy, to learn something about it, if you want to do something in it. But many would deny that what they do is derived from previous philosophy in a way they might grant that present-day painting or music are derived from their pasts, and not fully intelligible apart from them. Many philosophers say they are just interested in solving certain problems that present themselves, or in understanding certain phenomena, or putting forward correct theories of this or that aspect of the world. They are not concerned with what was said about such matters in the past, although they grant that others, even others in philosophy, might be interested in such questions.

W. V. Quine, for example, has remarked that people go into philosophy for different reasons: some are interested in the history of philosophy, and some are interested in philosophy. He would put himself in the second category. But the fact that Quine is not primarily interested in studying the history of philosophy does not mean that he philosophizes in ignorance of or in isolation from that tradition. In fact Quine knows a great deal about the history of philosophy. It is just that the history of philosophy for him was

Carnap, and *Principia Mathematica*. He knows both of them very well. His philosophy is in large part a response to them. There is a lot more of C. I. Lewis in it than he would care to admit, as well. The same sort of thing is true of any theorists who claim to be doing nothing more than directing their philosophically unfettered minds onto problematic aspects of a more or less neutrally describable public world.

There are many philosophical theorists, and philosophical theories and doctrines. That is to say, many philosophers describe what they are doing in those ways. What puzzled G. E. Moore was the relation between the kinds of things such philosophers say and facts of the everyday world that we all know. That seems to me to be the right kind of question to ask about those things called "philosophical theses" or "doctrines" or "results." What do they imply about what we all know, or about what is so, outside philosophy? Does "Time is unreal," for example, imply that I did not have my breakfast *after* I got out of bed, or not? And if it does, isn't it simply false, since I did get out of bed first this morning? I find it exhilarating when philosophers raise, and press, questions like this, even about so-called philosophical theories themselves.

I say this is the right kind of question to ask, or at least to start from, since it leads to questioning the very nature of a "philosophical" thesis or doctrine or theory. It is a way of pursuing our question "What is philosophy?," but from down on the ground, as it were, as it presents itself in particular real cases. This is not something that much concerns many of those who are busy producing, or at least seeking, theses or theories in philosophy. It seems to be very important to many philosophers to have some position or doctrine or theory with which to identify themselves. This now seems to dominate at least that part of philosophy that is conducted in English. Theories are constructed, or proposed, and philosophical discussion amounts to pitting these positions or theories against one another. It is apparently thought to be a virtue to stick by your theory as long as you can, making adjustments under pressure only if opposed theories seem to be gaining an advantage, and to keep trying to give your own position the best run for its money in the competitive marketplace.

This serves a professional enterprise very well. Each operator has his or her own niche in the subject, and so a certain professional identity. And the relative fortunes of each player's project can be charted to some extent. The whole picture appears to be modeled on a certain conception—no doubt a mythical conception—of how real science proceeds, with a further economic metaphor now added to the myth. One hears a lot in philosophy these days of "buying into" this or that theory or "ism" or "research program." When I first went to California in the flourishing 1960s, graduate students who found a new idea or suggestion promising might say "I'll buy that." Now the most they can afford is to buy "into" something. They are prepared to put what money they have into "anti-realism" versus "realism," say, or "externalism" versus "internalism," and then try to defend their investment against all comers.

This can sometimes lead to something new and worthwhile. Philosophy throughout its history has thrown off many questions and programs that have become self-sufficient subjects or even sciences of their own. A chair in physics in Oxford today is still called the chair of "Natural Philosophy." But it is not within the Sub-Faculty of Philosophy. This might be one thing that accounts for the fact that there are no results in philosophy: as soon as there are real results, it no longer counts as philosophy.

But I think the professionalized, scientistic conception that many people now have of how to proceed in philosophy is unfortunate. Despite many impressive achievements of sheer brain power, it remains, to my mind, unsatisfactory and, if not unphilosophical, at least not sufficiently philosophical. In the terms I used earlier, I would say that it is compatible at a certain point with the absence of philosophy. It has led to what I think is a certain complacency, even a certain blindness, in the face of what remains philosophically important. I don't mean that the best constructive theoretical philosophers are complacent in defense of their theories or blind to possibly damaging objections to them. But I think that in philosophical enterprise or penetration they tend to stop one step too soon. They are insufficiently critical of what a philosophical thesis or theory amounts to, and what it means to adopt or accept such a thing. That makes philosophical theorizing look too much like accepting an ideology or a creed or a religion. It does not take into philosophical consideration the very attitude of so-called acceptance itself, or the very status of the doctrines or theory accepted. It takes for granted that we understand what sort of thing a philosophical doctrine or theory is, and asks only which ones to accept and which to reject.

I find this unsatisfactory, or not sufficiently philosophical, because I think that what is then taken for granted is something we do not understand: what is this enterprise we philosophers are engaged in, and what can be expected from it? That is a form of the question "What is philosophy?," and it is a question for philosophy itself. Who else will address it? Philosophical theories about this or that aspect of the world do not address it. They are instances of the very thing it asks about. That is what we want to understand better than we do.

What philosophical theories or theses are, or what the answers to philosophical problems say or mean, can only be as clear and as well understood as the questions they answer or the phenomena they are meant to account for. But those problems, or the conceptions that give rise to them, are themselves the results of thought—of thinking of things in certain ways. And to understand those problems, even before trying to answer them, we have to identify and understand those ways of thinking, and assess them. But those ways of thinking are also at least in part the product of previous philosophizing, and that too we have to identify and understand. Only in this way, I think, can we come to know what we are doing in philosophy. We have to get at the sources of the so-called problems, to see where they come from and why they take the forms that they do. This is what I think is left out or simply taken as known by those who are busy answering the questions, solving the problems, or producing theories of heretofore problematic phenomena.

This is something I think we can no longer take for granted in philosophy. It is something that many theories since the time of Kant have tried to account for. Those theories by now have been repudiated. And rightly so. But putting scientistic slogans in their place is no advance. What we need now is a much closer look at what actually goes on. But not in general—in detail. We need to see where philosophical problems come from in order to understand the special character of what is said in attempts to solve them.

One word sometimes applied to the kind of philosophical attitude or curiosity I am recommending is *therapeutic*. The term is unfortunate, and does not capture what I have in mind. Wittgenstein does say that there are different methods in philosophy, "like different therapies."[3] But that might mean, allowing for the bad grammar, only that there are different methods in philosophy, just as there are different therapies in psychotherapy. That does not imply that the different ways of doing things in philosophy *are* therapies. On that reading, the remark means only the equivalent of "There is more than one way to skin a cat."

With a cat there is no obscurity or uncertainty about the goal: you either end up with a fully skinned cat or you don't. But what is the analogue, even in psychotherapy, of the skinned cat? And if you think in that case that you can identify in advance a clear goal that could be reached by several different therapeutic means, what is the parallel in philosophy? What goal are different methods in philosophy all designed to achieve? *Therapeutic* as a term puts too much weight on an identifiable outcome. I prefer the word *diagnostic*. What philosophers need now is a diagnosis or uncovering of what they regard as their problems or their questions, and some understanding of the nature and sources of the kinds of things they think philosophy should account for.

Wittgenstein also says, as translated by Elizabeth Anscombe: "The philosopher's treatment of a question is like the treatment of an illness."[4] This suggests that the philosopher, or the philosopher Wittgenstein approves of, treats a philosophical question like an illness—or even that he thinks a philosophical question is an illness. I think that is an unfortunate suggestion. The thing to do with an illness, after all, is to get rid of it. Hence the idea of therapy or cure. But, as we have just seen, Wittgenstein also says there are many different therapies, and you can get rid of something in lots of different ways. Why would "philosophical methods," if there are any, be any better than anything else that works? Best of all would be not to get the thing in the first place. And with philosophical questions, that can be arranged. So on this reading, Wittgenstein would be suggesting that nothing would be lost without philosophy.

I think Wittgenstein's remark should be taken in another way, which puts it much closer to the conception of philosophy or philosophical activity I think we now need—or need to resuscitate. It makes a place for philosophy. What Wittgenstein writes, in the German, is: "Der Philosoph behandelt eine Frage; wie eine Krankheit," which could be put something like this: "The philosopher treats a question; as an illness (is treated)." The stress is on the verb. The philosopher treats a question; the doctor *treats* an illness. The parallel is with what is done, not necessarily with what it is done to.

Well, how is an illness treated? First of all, and crucially, it has to be identified. "What have we got here, exactly," we ask, "and how does it differ from other things that are very similar but different?" These symptoms must then be diagnosed. What are they indications of? What lies behind them? How did things develop so that these symptoms show up in this form here and now? The time for therapy and cure can come only after these questions have been answered. The point is that treatment begins with identification and understanding, and an illness to be treated is understood in terms of its origins or causes. We understand what it is in terms of how it came to be.

Treating a question is not the same as answering it. Answering it might be the worst thing to do with it. I believe that happens in philosophy. Answering a question before understanding what it is and where it comes from is like applying a cure for an illness without having identified what illness it is. It can make things worse, and certainly harder to identify and understand. To understand what philosophical theses or theories are, we have to understand the nature and sources of the problems to which they are answers. And to understand those problems we have to identify and understand their sources.

I do not mean that we must always seek their temporal or historical sources. We need to identify the assumptions, the demands, the preconceptions, and the aspirations that lead to a question's having the particular significance it now has for us, but that need not mean going back to earlier stages of the philosophical tradition. The particular frame of mind that is responsible for the question is something we are in right now. That does not mean it is therefore easy to identify. But given that philosophy is always in part a response to previous philosophy, we can be pretty sure that the sources of questions that now lie within us, and to that extent seem uncontroversial, are the products of earlier philosophizing or earlier ways of thinking about the world. That is why I think philosophy is inseparable from the history of philosophy. But not every particular attempt to plumb the sources of a philosophical problem must take us backward in time. The important thing is to gain some understanding of the origin and special character of the problem or issue right now, whatever that takes.

So philosophical investigation as I think of it should extend in this way to the process or activity of philosophy itself. An unrelenting self-consciousness is essential to the task. I think only the application of philosophical self-reflection to the very procedures and products of self-reflection can reveal what philosophy is, or what it can offer. But there always has to be something more to reflect on, or to start from, than just the activity of philosophizing itself. There has to be something we think, something we are trying to understand, some puzzling phenomenon or aspect of the world. There must be some "data," so to speak, to reflect on, or to come to terms with, even if they are only the way a problem presents itself to us, or a felt need to understand things in a certain way. There must be some things we know, or things that are so, or things that we think and cannot deny, that are firmer than anything that philosophical theorizing can undermine.

I don't mean anything here like "foundations" of knowledge, or "self-evident truths." I mean facts, convictions, or attitudes that we are engaged with as mature thinkers and agents in a public world—something we are involved in, or subject to, as active, feeling, human beings, and which philosophy is presumably in some way meant to help illuminate. There must be some things which, in Thomas Nagel's phrase, we "think straight." There must be something we are involved in that is not philosophy. In reflecting on such things philosophically we have to have the strength to recognize and hold on to such things, and not to distort or deny them, in the face of philosophical reflection. Otherwise, whatever importance or interest philosophical thought can have is lost.

This is what I find admirable about G. E. Moore, for all his limitations in recognizing what a philosophical attack on such things might be up to. There is virtually no philosophical diagnosis in Moore; there is just the steadfast insistence that this is true, that is false, and that we all know such-and-such. On its own, as it appears in Moore, that can be philosophically dissatisfying; it can seem shallow and uncomprehending. But without some such engagement and steadfastness about something, without something we unshakably think to be so, at least at the time, philosophical self-reflection on its own becomes vulnerable to complete self-absorption—what Christopher Ricks has called "narcissistic regression." If we focus only on the things we are inclined to say now, and why we are inclined to say them, and why we are inclined to say that about our present inclination, and so on, we are left with mere play. We have nothing to think about except the rhetorical effects of the rhetorical devices we have employed in previous responses. We would then have lost the connection between our thinking and anything else in the world, especially anything that matters. That really would be, again in Ricks's words, a kind of "kamikaze of the intellect."[5]

So I think that in philosophy we have to look at each problem or issue or phenomenon, and respond to it authentically as it presents itself to us at the time, without denying or dismissing what we honestly cannot deny or dismiss. We cannot simply accept it without scrutiny, and we cannot simply declare the problem bogus or the alleged phenomenon illusory on the basis of some quite general theoretical belief about the contrived or contingent sources of philosophical problems. We have to take the particular issue as seriously as we can bring ourselves to feel it. We have to participate in, not just comment on, philosophical thought.

Barry Stroud

If we do that, what do we get? Or what can we expect? Again, I think nothing illuminating can be said in general terms. If we hold on to our attachment to the world, what we can hope for in a particular case is at least a sharper awareness, and so a fuller appreciation, of the detail and complexity of those aspects of the everyday world that gave rise to philosophical reflection about them. By seeing the distortions, or even perhaps the impossibility, of a detached, theoretical account of something, we might come to appreciate better what the philosophical enterprise aspires to. To see how and why we can never achieve such a point of view on the world might provide its own kind of human or self-understanding—perhaps the best or the only kind we can really hope for.

But for any of this to be possible—and this is my main point—we have to *participate* in the activity of philosophy. There is no shortcut, and no formula. So to the completely general, detached question "What is philosophy?" I say "Don't ask; don't tell." It is a question to be treated, not answered. Trying to answer it in that general form gets you nowhere. You have to look at some particular bit of philosophy, or better still *do* some philosophy—think about something, and try to get to the bottom of it—and then ask yourself what is going on. "What is really being said and done here," we have to ask, "and what does it imply about this or that undeniable fact of the world?" I think philosophy promises most only if you do this each time the philosophical urge arises, or each time a philosophical issue comes along. This is especially true when it comes along in your own thoughts, and in your own voice.

Notes

1. André Malraux, *The Voices of Silence*, trans. Stuart Gilbert (Princeton: Princeton University Press, 1978), 281.

2. G. E. Moore, "Autobiography," in *The Philosophy of G. E. Moore,* ed. Paul A. Schilpp (La Salle: Open Court, 1968), 14.

3. Ludwig Wittgenstein, *Philosophical Investigations,* trans. G. E. M. Anscombe (New York: Macmillan, 1953), §133.

4. Ibid., §255.

5. Christopher Ricks, *T. S. Eliot and Prejudice* (London: Faber and Faber, 1994), 21, 90.

Barry Stroud

2

Philosophy in Search of Itself

Karsten Harries

Wh at is philosophy? The question suggests a certain uneasiness on the part of philosophers. Chemists don't arrange symposia with the title "What is chemistry?" Astronomers don't arrange symposia with the title "What is astronomy?" Artists, on the other hand, today are even more preoccupied than philosophers with just what it is they are doing. Does the very title of our symposium then suggest that in important ways philosophy today is closer to art than to astronomy? Once, to be sure, things were different. In their origin astronomy and philosophy are intertwined: Thales, the first philosopher, was also an astronomer. Why should there now be such a gap between them, a gap between philosophy and science?

What is philosophy? The answer should be easy. All the speakers here are philosophers. For a first answer, then, we may look at the kind of work philosophers engage in. And what is that? Harry Frankfurt once insisted that "The only irrevocable commitment that the philosopher has is to the truth, or if you don't like that, to some sort of disciplined, self-controlled inquiry into a vague set, vaguely defined set of issues that are identified as philosophical. That's what he's supposed to do."[1] But who here is doing the identifying and supposing? And just what is it that the philosopher is supposed to do? The first formulation—"The only irrevocable commitment that the philosopher has is to the truth"—does not offer much of a pointer. Are philosophers more committed to the truth than, say, astronomers or biologists? If philosophers are indeed committed, not just to truth, but to *the* truth, it would seem that the many truths science or history pursues will not do. The philosopher is looking for some more essential truth. But just what is that truth? Presumably not a truth concerning the inner makeup of some star or the mechanism of reproduction, even if these are issues that once very much concerned philosophers. Today we would turn to scientists for answers to such problems, a reminder that our understanding of the task of the philosopher is inevitably shadowed by the progress of science, which has assumed responsibility for much that once concerned philosophers. Just as the development of photography has called into question any understanding of art as a representation of nature, so the development of natural science has called into question any understanding of philosophy as a representation of reality. We no longer turn to philosophy to learn what is the case. If the philosopher today is indeed committed to the truth, presumably this truth is quite different from that pursued by science.

But how important is truth to most philosophers? When I pick a new kind of mushroom for supper, I try to make sure that I have not picked some poisonous specimen. In such cases, being right may be quite literally a matter of life and death. Are the stakes ever that high for the philosopher? But perhaps that has to do with the kind of truth that concerns him, a truth quite different from the merely ontic truths that matter to us in everyday life and that matter to scientists.

But is it really the possession of the truth that matters most to philosophers? After all, such possession would put them out of work, would be the end of philosophy. Their work would be done. In this sense, as Kierkegaard remarked, the promised completion of the Hegelian system once threatened the end of philosophy, and it was with Hegel in mind that he cited Lessing's words: "If God had locked up all truth in his right hand, and in his left the unique, ever-live striving for truth, albeit with the addition that I should always and eternally err, and he said to me 'Choose!', I should humbly clasp his left hand, saying: 'Father, give. Pure truth is after all for thee alone.' "[2] Thoughts of a philosophy finally in possession of the truth, of the completed system, the finished architecture of truth, are inevitably, as Bachelard says of thoughts of the finally built dream house, "serious, sad thoughts. . . . It is better to live in a state of impermanence than in one of finality."[3] Is the philosopher perhaps so interested in *the* truth because it forever eludes him? Nietzsche suggests something of the sort when he praises Lessing, this "most honest theoretical man," for having "dared to announce that he cared more for the search after the truth than for the truth itself."[4]

But does even the search after the truth matter to philosophers? Responding to Frankfurt, Richard Rorty suggests that what matters to philosophers is less the pursuit of truth than "the free and open exchange of opinions."[5] Is it perhaps freedom, the freedom of this play of opinions, that matters more to the philosopher than the possession of truth? But must such a free and open exchange not degenerate into intellectual game-playing unless in some sense bound? Bound to the truth? Just what is at issue in such play? Frankfurt points to the difficulty we face when he insists that philosophers are committed to "self-controlled inquiry into a vague set, vaguely defined set of issues that are identified as philosophical." Even that, Rorty retorts, claims too much: "I don't think there is a clear range of things called philosophical problems."[6]

We have been moving in a circle: the issues that concern philosophers are philosophical. What is philosophy?

The Philosophy World

I wonder whether there is a substantive definition of philosophy on which all the contributors to this volume could agree. To be sure, something like a first answer to our question is suggested by the fact that we have all been invited to contribute to this book as philosophers. How did those issuing the invitations know how to recognize us? The answer seems obvious: all of us here have earned a Ph.D. in philosophy, a kind of plumber's license that allows us to ply our trade, to teach philosophy. All of us are in the business of philosophy, members of universities and of such professional organizations as the American Philosophical Association. Does such membership make me a philosopher? In some sense it surely does. This is how I make a living: as a philosopher, teaching and writing philosophy.

But must we not distinguish between the philosophy teacher and the genuine philosopher? In a recent survey of American philosophy, Nicholas Rescher draws just such a distinction, defining philosophers as "active contributors to the intellectual resource of the discipline."[7] This comes close to defining the philosopher as a professor of philosophy who also publishes in his field, a definition that, Rescher points out, is growing obsolete because of "a growing professionalism based on more rigorous formal training and a 'publish or perish' ethics in the academy" that "has meant that the teaching staffs in American colleges are increasingly populated by people who are productive philosophers."[8]

What makes you a productive philosopher in this sense is that you publish, ideally in refereed journals. This is a necessary condition of promotion to tenure at our better institutions. Today the question: "What is philosophy?" receives thus a first answer from the philosophy establishment. This suggests an institutional theory of philosophy parallel to Arthur Danto's and George Dickie's institutional theory of art. According to Danto, "Something is a work of art when decreed to be such by a loose constellation of individuals who are defined by their institutional identities to be within something called 'the art world': curators, art writers, collectors, dealers, and, of course, artists themselves who, for whatever reasons, put forward certain objects as candidates for assessment as works of art."[9] Analogously, something would be a work of philosophy when decreed to be such by a loose constellation of individuals who are defined by their institutional identities to be within something we might call the philosophy world: university administrators, book reviewers and journal referees, editors, students, and, of course, the philosophers themselves who, for whatever reasons, put forward certain views and writings as candidates for assessment as philosophy. And just as the institutional theory of art belongs with an art no longer committed to some master narrative of what art has been and should be, so the institutional theory of philosophy answers to a philosophy world no longer united by a substantive understanding of what philosophy has been and should be.

Just as the lack of a substantive understanding of what art should be has been no obstacle to a still vigorous art production, so the lack of a shared, substantive understanding of what philosophy should be would seem to have been no obstacle to the flourishing of American philosophy, which, as Rescher suggests in his report "today is characterized not by uniformity and cohesion but by a luxuriant diversity that offers something to suit most every taste."[10] As Rescher describes it, American philosophy is not held together by a shared understanding of philosophy and the philosopher's task. "Such unity as American philosophy affords is that of an academic industry, not that of a single doctrinal orientation or school."[11]

Philosophy has become an industry, a business, a trade. There is tension between such an understanding of philosophy and Frankfurt's insistence that the philosopher's only irrevocable commitment is to the truth, the latter inviting an understanding of philosophy as for philosophy's sake, requiring a freedom of thought difficult to reconcile with industrial production.

Can we bring these two determinations together and understand philosophy as the business of truth production? Which returns us to the question "What kind of truth?" and leaves one wondering why society should support such a strange business. And that society does support the philosophy business—if perhaps not nearly to the degree, or as lavishly, as philosophers might like or think they deserve—is demonstrated by every APA meeting. As Rescher observes, the "most striking feature" of American philosophy "at this historic juncture [1992] is its scope and scale."[12] The APA has more than eight thousand members, the *Directory of American Philosophers* lists over ten thousand names—less than twenty percent women, less than two percent minorities.

If Rescher is right, the professionalization of philosophy has led to a welcome raising of standards. "Considering the quantity of philosophical writing that sees the light of print, its overall quality is respectably high—that is if one's standard gives weight to the technical dimension (Depth of insight is another matter). At any rate the day of the philosopher as isolated thinker—the talented amateur with an idiosyncratic message—is effectively gone. For better or for worse, an outsider along the lines of a Spinoza or a Nietzsche would find it near to impossible to get a hearing in the North American philosophical world today."[13] It isn't just a matter of the absence of philosophers in the image of Socrates. The professionalization of philosophy has meant a general leveling of the philosophical playing field. No longer are there a few giants dominating the philosophical scene as they did in the Germany of the nineteenth century. There is no modern Hegel. With Wittgenstein and Heidegger, the age of the great philosophers seems to have come to an end. And this appears more than an unfortunate accident: the spiritual situation of our age would seem to deny room to such philosophers. Karl-Otto Apel has claimed that "the category of 'the great thinkers'" has become a thing of the past.[14] And should we mourn that our approach to philosophy has become less monological, less solipsistic—that in philosophy, too, the team is beginning to replace the solitary individual?

Such insistence on teamwork has consequences for the style of philosophy. Much as a work like Heidegger's *Beiträge* still fascinates some of our philosophers, does it not represent the kind of monological thinking philosophy has happily left behind? Heidegger to be sure had a very different understanding of the nature of philosophical thought. In a letter to Jaspers, who had called for a dialogical philosophy, he countered: "Much, however, would have been gained if monologues were allowed to remain what they are. It almost seems to me that they are not yet [genuine monologues]. For that they are not yet strong enough."[15]

To us, as to Jaspers, such supposed strength, so intimately bound up with "the category of 'the great thinkers'," is likely to seem a temptation. Rescher observes that "If the development of American philosophy continues along its present path, the role of the individual, as seen in the historiography of the future, will be as the subject of a footnote illustrative of the diversified genera, trends and tendencies of thought to which the main body of the text will have to be dedicated."[16] We expect the philosopher to present himself or herself as a member of an ongoing working community, expect published work to make reference to (preferably recent) literature that supports or challenges what is being asserted. What philosopher today gets away with the stance communicated by the style of Spinoza's *Ethics* or Wittgenstein's *Tractatus*, where the special appeal of such style is tied to the way it turns a cold shoulder to demands for easy communicability and seems to celebrate mono-logical thinking?

Not that the prevailing style of philosophical work today invites a broad readership. It rather tends to present such work as part of a philosophical conversation going on among small groups of sim-ilarly interested professionals working in the ivory towers of our colleges and universities. Apel has spoken of "the institutionaliza-tion of human communication." The institutionalization of com-munication that is so much part of today's philosophy world—just think of e-mail and the internet—does not mean that some names do not still count more than others. To cite Rescher once more: "Scattered here and there in separated castles, prominent individ-uals gain a local following of loyal friends or enemies. But no one among the academic philosophers of today manages to impose his agenda on more than a minimal fraction of the large, internally diversified community. Even the most influential of contemporary American philosophers is simply yet another—somewhat larger—fish in a very populous sea."[17]

An Academic Industry

If the disappearance of the philosophical genius, the solitary great thinker, would appear to be one casualty of the professional-ization of philosophy, abetted by advances in transportation and communication, equally significant is a second feature of today's philosophy world: agenda enlargement. According to Rescher, "Theory diversity and doctrinal dissonance are the order of the day, and the only evident interconnection is that of geographic prox-imity. . . . Every doctrine, every theory, every approach finds its devotees somewhere within the overall community. On most of the larger issues there are no significant majorities." Rescher does go on to chronicle a number of trends, the most significant among them the rise in historical studies—by 1992 one third of all Ph.D. dissertations in this country dealt primarily with historical issues.[18]

Let me return to Rescher's description of philosophy today as a substantial industry with "a prolific and diversified range of products"—like all the humanities a bit on the defensive, to be sure, as shown by the decline of doctorates awarded each year,[19] but still offering reasonable (though diminishing) employment opportunities and compensating for comparatively low pay with considerable free time. As Rescher points out, a hundred flowers are allowed to bloom in the American philosophy world: Entire societies "are dedicated to the pursuit of issues, now deemed philosophical, that no one would have dreamt of considering so a generation ago. Some examples are the Society for Machines and Mentality, for Informal Logic and Critical Thinking, for the Study of Ethics and Animals, for Philosophy and Literature, for Analytical Feminism, and for the Philosophy of Sex and Love. The fact that those many hundreds of philosophers are looking for something to do that is not simply a matter of re-exploring familiar ground has created a substantial population pressure for more philosophical *Lebensraum*."[20]

Philosophical *Lebensraum* means room for philosophers to make a living. That room is granted first of all by institutions of higher learning, which in turn are dependent on and must therefore be responsive to the larger community. Such dependence inevitably threatens the freedom of thought that a philosopher like Schopenhauer took to be a presupposition of philosophy. "How could philosophy," Schopenhauer challenges us professional philosophers, "degraded to become a means of earning one's bread, generally fail to degenerate into sophistry? Just because this is bound to happen, and the rule 'I sing the song of him whose bread I eat' has held good at all times, the making of money by philosophy was among the ancients the characteristic of the sophist. We have to still add that, since everywhere in this world nothing is to be expected, nothing can be demanded, and nothing is to be had for money except mediocrity, we have to put up with this here also."[21]

That academic institutions tend to be slow to change has no doubt benefited philosophers, given the growing indifference of the society at large to philosophy. Such indifference is reflected, as Rescher reports, by the fact that in 1977 the *Encyclopedia Britannica*'s *Book of the Year* discontinued coverage of what happened in philosophy, that *Who's Who in America* drastically curtailed its coverage of philosophers, and that *Time* and the *New York Times* lamented philosophy's irrelevance even while philosophers attempted to make philosophy more relevant (think of the evolution of medical, business, and environmental ethics). "With relish" philosophers have turned to "the problems on the agenda of public policy and personal concern."[22] "Refreshingly free of ideological commitments," American philosophy addresses "palpable problems by whatever means lie to hand, relying on the power of intellectual technology to carry the day."[23] Rescher considers it "one of those ironies not uncommon in the pages of history" that philosophy should have returned "to the issues of the day at almost the very moment when the wider public gave up thinking of the discipline as relevant to its concerns."[24]

The Philosopher as Plumber

Viewing philosophy pragmatically as something like an intellectual technology, Richard Rorty has invited us to look at the work of a philosopher like Heidegger as a "toolbox" we have inherited, "containing a very varied assortment, constructed for various different purposes—an assortment in which only some items are still useful."[25] This raises the question of what here provides the criterion for what makes some items useful. Rorty's answer: "usefulness for American liberalism."[26] Is "American liberalism," then, beyond question? If a certain activity or way of life can be taken for granted and is placed beyond challenge, we may well want to consider the philosopher a kind of intellectual plumber, a professional called on to fix certain problems in what is our social home.

Think of applied ethics, of today's "ethicists." The term invites questioning: "ist" derives from the Greek *istes,* forming agent-nouns from verbs ending in *izein.* A baptist is thus someone who baptizes, a plagiarist someone who plagiarizes. An ethicist accordingly would be someone who "ethicizes," a rare word meaning "to discuss ethics; to speak or write on morals, moralize," a word that— so the *Oxford English Dictionary* informs us—usually carries a negative connotation (like the word *edify*). The ethicist would then be a specialist who, having mastered his craft, is now prepared to address ethical problems wherever they appear.

Unfortunately, as its uncertain history demonstrates, ethics has not managed to establish itself as a secure science. That failure testifies to the inability of pure reason to establish ethics on a firm foundation. Inevitably today's ethicists recall the Greek sophists. It is easy to understand the desire for experts able to deal with the ethical dimension of the difficult problems that arise in everyday life, and especially in the different professions—problems for which most professionals have too little time and which they are ill trained to address. Ethicists might thus free other professionals to devote themselves more fully to what they are truly experts in. The gain seems evident.

But should moral responsibility be left to experts? To be sure, the professionalization of ethics is quite in keeping with the ethos of this age of the specialist, which has seen a splintering of the life of the individual into different roles and tasks and often ephemeral groupings, weakening the communal foundation on which an effective civic ethics must rest. Be professional! That all too often means: don't let your all-too-human misgivings, doubts, and questions—

and especially your moral hang-ups—prevent you from acting professionally.

Here are some examples: imagine a pilot asked to drop bombs or fire rockets that, he knows, will kill innocent people. Would it not be in the military's interest to make sure that our pilot, should his conscience give him sleepless nights, could consult with an ethicist, who (by invoking some greater good) could justify to him this particular war and mission with its inevitable loss of life, who would allow him to get the rest he so desperately needs to perform his appointed task, who might agree that "war is hell" but would remind him that "war is war" and demands of the professional warrior that he bracket himself as a whole human being?

Similar considerations apply in industry. Say some mine in New Guinea can be opened up only at the price of the destruction of the way of life of some quite unimportant tribe, a tribe very few people will even have heard of—and they are cannibals, to boot! Would it not be comforting for some C.E.O., kept awake by his conscience, to be able to speak to an ethicist his firm had hired, a thoughtful recent Ph.D. from one of our best programs in business ethics, an eloquent young person able to prove to him that his actions advanced the cause of the greatest good of the greatest number and are therefore justified, that he need not burden himself with guilt feelings? "You have to break eggs to make an omelet," and anyway, "business is business."

The situation is more difficult for the doctor, who professionally committed to care for human beings is yet forced by his very profession to focus, specialize, and economize in ways that make it difficult for him to remain open to the whole human being, let alone to the suffering of countless human beings who must go without adequate care. As a professional he, too, will have to acknowledge that time is money, will be governed by considerations often difficult to reconcile with the requirements of healing. Should such a doctor not welcome an ethicist in his hospital, an expert there to lift at least some of the burden of moral responsibility off the shoulders of our already-harried doctor, to help make our doctor a bit less anxious?

But is it the task of philosophy to free us from anxiety? Could it be, as Heidegger suggested in his Davos debate with Cassirer, that its task is just the opposite: to make us more anxious; not to lift the burden of personal responsibility, but to make it weigh more heavily?[27] Could it be that anxiety is the price of genuine freedom and that one task of philosophy is to free us? I am suspicious of ethicists to the extent that they understand their task (in the image of Abigail van Buren) to be that of solving life problems, and thereby reducing anxiety. And I am suspicious of professional ethics insofar as it seeks to lighten the burden of responsibility borne by our often already overburdened professionals. My recent *The Ethical Function of Architecture* therefore makes no attempt to tell architects what to do. Instead it tries to call into question—and thus to free architects from—an often-taken-for-granted understanding of architecture as an art, albeit an essentially unchaste art, unchaste because it has always already sold itself to the world. To such an understanding the book opposes its insistence on architecture's ethical function, where the meaning of *ethical* is thought, following Heidegger, in the light of the Greek *ethos,* which refers to a person's character or disposition, his placement, together with others, in the world. In this fundamental sense architecture cannot help but have an ethical function. Architecture inevitably places human beings. Every architect therefore bears responsibility for how human beings are to exist in a shared world, for all building not only presupposes and makes visible an already established way of life; it inevitably helps to preserve, re-enforce, or challenge it, and thus helps shape the future. I should be pleased if my book makes the burden of such responsibility weigh just a bit more heavily on at least a few architects.

And does philosophy, too, not have such an ethical, place-establishing function? Once again it has become fashionable to think of the philosopher in the image of the architect, as a would-be builder, someone who edifies, where the very word *edify* should make us think. Once it meant simply to raise a dwelling or structure, later it came to mean "to improve morally or spiritually," and now it tends to carry a negative connotation. The word thus invites us to think not just about the simile that joins architecture and philosophy, but also about attacks on architecture that have recently come into fashion. What, for example, are we to make of the vogue enjoyed by the word *deconstruction* and all it stands for? What of invocations of Georges Bataille's stance against architecture?[28] Architecture here stands for an order that imprisons us and should be destroyed, even if such destruction threatens chaos and bestiality. The kind of reasoning that here makes the prison the paradigmatic work of architecture, a kind of lens through which to look at all architecture, is of the sort that lets Dostoevsky's Man from the Underground call twice-two-makes-four a piece of impudence and celebrate twice-two-makes-five as the ultimate refuge of a freedom that, resisting placement, dreams of labyrinth and chaos.[29] Although themselves claiming something like an ethical significance, attacks on architecture so understood are inevitably also attacks on all philosophy that claims to have raised a spiritual architecture that would assign human beings their proper place. Freedom resists such placement.

Loss of Way

In the *Philosophical Investigations,* Wittgenstein suggests that philosophical problems have the form "I do not know my way about."[30] To be sure, not all problems having this form are therefore already philosophical. To lose one's way on a hike is not sufficient to make one a philosopher; nor is failure to understand a new piece of equipment. Say my computer misbehaves and I don't know what to do; I don't know my way about. But such a loss of way does not present us with a philosophical problem. Why not? I would suggest that it fails to do so because in such cases our disorientation is only superficial. In a deeper sense we still know where we are, know our way and what to do. For example, in the first case I might ask some fellow hiker for directions or study a map. The problem here poses itself against a background of established and accepted ways of doing things to which we can turn to help us decide what is to be done. The terrain has already been charted.

Genuinely philosophical problems, as I understand them, have no such background. They are born of a deeper anxiety, a more profound uncertainty. It is therefore hardly surprising that philosophical reflection should flourish when traditions disintegrate and as a result human beings are forced to question the place assigned to them by nature, society, and history; searching for firmer ground, they demand that this place be more securely established. Those secure in the knowledge of their place have little need for philosophy, just as those who think themselves at home are not likely to suffer from homesickness. Philosophy, as I understand it, has its origin in a sense of homelessness that is intimately linked to the demand for authenticity, the demand that the individual should act and think for himself or herself—a demand that stands in some tension with today's professionalization of philosophy. At the center of philosophy so understood lies something like an ethical concern, born of the demand that individuals assume responsibility for their thoughts and actions, and of the consequent refusal to rest content with what has come to be established, accepted, and taken for granted. The demand for autonomy puts into question the authority of history or of the place nature has supposedly assigned to us, puts into question also the authority of philosophy. Philosophy is thus a critical, and especially a self-critical enterprise. Not that it can draw on a firm understanding of where to go. Quite the contrary: philosophy remains alive only as long as the question "What is the right way?" continues to be asked because that way remains questionable, because our place and vocation remains uncertain. Were philosophy to determine or decide on the right way, were it able to raise that house which allows for genuine dwelling, it would have done its work and come to an end. This is why the birth of a science has meant so often the death of a part of philosophy. Science is defined at least in part by a determination of what constitutes the right way or proper method. A scientist who calls that way into question returns to the philosophical origin of science.

As should be expected, given an understanding of philosophy as a pursuit of the truth, part of philosophy are dreams of a philosophy to end philosophy. Descartes thus thought the project of philosophy near completion, the architecture that he hoped to raise not far from finished; similarly Kant concludes his *Critique of Pure Reason* with an expression of hope that the desire to know, which had ruled philosophy for so many centuries, would (before the end of the eighteenth century) finally be satisfied and laid to rest once and for all; and realization of the Hegelian system would have meant the end of philosophy. I do not need here to show once more what has already been shown so often: that all these architectures turned out to be versions of the Tower of Babel, that philosophy continued to live.

Dislocation, Freedom, Wonder

Wittgenstein's suggestion that philosophical problems have the form "I do not know my way about" recalls Aristotle's identification of the origin of philosophy in wonder. However, Wittgenstein's remark communicates nostalgia for a homecoming that would mean also both escape from freedom and the end of philosophy (though

Wittgenstein thought such a home must be founded on ordinary language rather than philosophy), while Aristotle turns his account of the origin of philosophy into a celebration of free inquiry. "It is owing to their wonder that men both now begin and at first began to philosophize; they wondered originally at obvious difficulties, then advanced little by little and stated difficulties about the greater matters, e. g. about the phenomena of the moon and those of the sun and the stars, and about the genesis of the universe."[31] Philosophy here, too, is said to have its origin in those familiar dislocations or derailments that are part of everyday experience: we find ourselves stuck in some place; or we have lost our way, or we cannot find something we need to complete some task. We all run into difficulties that prevent us from just going on with whatever we were doing—that force us to pause, take a step back in order to determine just where we have come from, where we are, what possibilities are open to us, and what should be done. Note how such derailments open us to possibilities that remain unconsidered as long as life is on track. By opening up possibilities, they also open us to our freedom. Dislocation, freedom, and wonder belong together. To say philosophy has its origin in wonder is to say also that its beginning is the awakening of freedom. Only a free being is capable of wonder.

There is of course a decisive difference between such "obvious difficulties" and "the greater matters" that according to Aristotle concern the philosopher. While these "obvious difficulties" receive their significance from projects that are part of life, Aristotle's "greater matters" are pursued only to escape from ignorance, only for the sake of truth. Frankfurt may have had Aristotle in mind when he insisted that the philosopher's "only irrevocable commitment . . . is to the truth." So understood, the philosopher's commitment to pursue truth only for truth's sake implies a leave-taking from the everyday world and its concerns; there is a sense in which the philosopher stands in this world as an outsider, as Plato took pains to show with his descriptions of Socrates: although placed in Athens, belonging to it by birth and upbringing, Socrates yet transcends such belonging, transcends himself as the Athenian he knows himself to be, just because he is a philosopher. Such self-transcendence is inseparable from the freedom that defines philosophy and its search for truth. Philosophy is an exercise in freedom.

That the first philosopher should also have been the first absentminded philosopher is therefore no accident. I am referring, of course, to the anecdote Socrates tells in Plato's *Theaetetus* of the pretty Thracian servant girl who mocked Thales for falling into a well while gazing at the mysteries of the sky. Did he not have better things to look at? Socrates tells this story to illustrate what I have called the self-transcendence of the philosopher; in Plato's words, to show that only the "outer form" of the philosopher is in the city; the "mind, disdaining the littlenesses and nothingnesses of human things is 'flying all abroad'; as Pindar says, measuring earth and heaven and the things which are under and on the earth and above the heaven, interrogating the whole nature of each in all their entirety, but not condescending to anything which is within reach."[32] The philosopher reaches for what is not within his reach. Does he overreach?

We may well wonder whether thus "flying all abroad," looking for higher truths, the philosopher does not become another Icarus, who trades the home given to us humans for no home at all. Aristotle himself asks whether the kind of knowledge sought by philosophy should not be regarded beyond human power: "for in many ways human nature is in bondage, so that according to Simonides 'God alone can have this privilege,' and it is unfitting that man should not be content to seek the knowledge that is suited to him."[33] The philosopher's search for knowledge would make him the rival of God. But Aristotle dismisses the suggestion of hubris: God is not jealous; nor is such inquiry unnatural, for "all men by nature desire to know," and not because such knowledge might prove useful or help them find the right way; the pursuit of knowledge is not in need of such justification; it is its own reward. Without such autotelic activities life would be empty.

On this view the dignity of philosophy is inseparably bound up with its uselessness. Because it is not an industry or a business, because it is not good for anything else, but "exists for its own sake," philosophy is said by Aristotle to be "the only free science" and as such the worthy occupation of free human beings. Both Plato and Aristotle insist on this connection between philosophy and freedom: not only does the pursuit of philosophy require free time— only a person of leisure can be a philosopher—but it is precisely because the philosopher does not approach things and issues with a particular end in mind that he is able to see them with more open eyes. Freedom is a presupposition of truth. Born of freedom, philosophy liberates. That is why it belongs at the very center of a truly liberal education. Like freedom, philosophy is inseparable from our humanity.

Bound Freedom

I called philosophy both a pursuit of truth and an exercise in freedom. There is tension between these two determinations. The exercise of freedom is said to be the pursuit of what binds freedom. But does freedom remain freedom when thus bound? Some philosophers have seen no great difficulty here: Descartes, e. g., insists that the will binds itself willingly and freely to whatever it clearly knows and thereby perfects itself and comes to rest. And similarly according to Kant freedom perfects itself when it binds itself to the rule of reason.

But is such perfection of freedom not also its death? Consider this passage from Kant's *Foundations:* "The rational being must regard himself always as legislative in a realm of ends possible through the freedom of the will, whether he belongs to it as member or as sovereign."[34] But this rational being who must so regard himself is at some distance from that being I am, bound to the body, and possessed of a different sort of freedom that reveals itself in the question: Why be moral? This freedom does not belong to human beings insofar as they are members of the kingdom of ends, but to the solitary individual who places himself higher than the universal, who experiences what Kant calls our membership in the kingdom of ends as problematic, as something he can refuse. Kant would call such a refusal evil. But the very possibility of evil forces us to question any too intimate association of freedom with Kant's practical reason. Freedom is disposed not just to the good, but also to evil. But perhaps we should say: ours is a freedom beyond good and evil. This freedom calls into question the authority of pure practical reason. Kantian autonomy here is transformed into existentialist authenticity, which does not recognize a transcendent measure of human actions, a God who created human beings in his image—which recognizes that God is dead. This would seem to leave the subject's own radical freedom as the only source of value.

But divorced from the ability to respond to what already claims us, freedom loses all content and evaporates. Our finite freedom means also such ability to respond, means response-ability in this sense. Our finite freedom, however, is haunted by the possibility of a more radical, godlike freedom. But this is a temptation: freedom alone lacks the strength to found values. If value had its foundation just in human freedom, a person who found life without meaning could cure himself or herself just by an act of will. Values or meanings cannot finally be willed, cannot be freely invented; they must be discovered.

Self-affirmation requires that freedom be bound. But what always has already bound freedom is the body, which limits our possibilities, our access to reality, and even our reason: unless mediated by the body, reason's claims remain hollow. Consider once more the spiritual architecture raised by Kant's ethics. Supposedly founded only in reason, his categorical imperative bids us treat all rational beings as ends in themselves. But this presupposes that we are able to recognize and respond to persons, that we are able to experience other human beings as worthy of respect. Moral responsibility presupposes such response-ability. This is of course a platitude, but a platitude sufficient to show that any understanding of experience that reduces the self to a thinking subject and reality to mute facts that lack meaning until endowed by that subject with meaning does violence to our experience of both persons and things. To the embodied self experiencing care and desire, reality gives itself first of all as always already charged with meaning. Every time we recognize another human being, we experience the incarnation of meaning in matter as a living reality. Without such experiences of meaning incarnated in matter, moral precepts would be without application and life meaningless. To repeat: freedom must be bound to such response-ability.

The Task of Philosophy

I spoke of experiences of meaning incarnated in matter as the ground of the moral life. But even talk of such an incarnation seems at odds with that commitment to objectivity that is a presupposition of the scientist's pursuit of truth. That pursuit had to lead to a reduction of reality to a collection of mute facts, raw material that lacks meaning until appropriated and put to use by human subjects. Science so understood knows nothing of incarnations of meaning in matter, knows nothing of freedom, knows therefore nothing of persons as persons. Technology has carried that reduction into our everyday life, inviting us to look not just at the earth, but also at persons, including ourselves—especially our bodies—as material to be used and shaped as we see fit. This is why science presents philosophy today with what I take to be its most pressing problem, a problem that—since science, too, has its origin in freedom—is but a timely expression of philosophy's endless attempt to think its own origin and essence.

Freedom gives an open mind, allows us to see things as they are. But ours is a finite freedom: we are bound just by having the senses and bodies we do have. Whatever we experience we experience from a particular perspective, where reflection just on this simple fact is sufficient to establish a first distinction between appearance and reality. Subject to perspective, we are imprisoned in a world of appearances, cut off from the truth. How then do we gain access to this reality? Precisely by freeing our understanding from the relativity of perspective. Objectivity demands freedom from all sorts of perspectival distortions. The truth of scientific propositions may thus be conceived as a correspondence to these objects, where it is important to keep in mind that these objects are not given to the senses, but must be reconstructed in thought. Such reconstruction is the task of science. And there is no reason to think that such reconstruction should or ever could be fully adequate to these objects, which function as regulative ideals. Though truth, so understood, is correspondence, the *test* of truth turns out to be coherence. Coherence here means more than the fit of such a reconstruction with our other relevant judgments; to commit oneself to the pursuit of truth so understood is to commit oneself also to the freedom of those who join us in this pursuit.

This quite ordinary understanding of the meaning of truth as correspondence—*pace* Heidegger, far older than Plato—is sufficient to allow us to claim an unambiguous sense in which science has progressed since the Greeks.[35] The measure of that progress is given just by the idea of objectivity. The progressive securing of the method or way to be taken by this pursuit has meant also the progressive emancipation of science from the tutelage of philosophy.

I therefore cannot agree with Alvin Plantinga when, divorcing science from the commitment to objectivity, he claims that "What the Christian community really needs is a science that takes into account what we know as Christians."[36] A Christian science is not what we need; is not what the Christian community needs. Science cannot let go of its commitment to objectivity. Ernan McMullin is right to insist that this "methodological naturalism does not restrict our study of nature; it just lays down which sort of study qualifies as scientific. If someone wants to pursue another approach to nature and there are many others—the methodological naturalist has no reason to object. Scientists have to proceed in this way."[37] A Christian science is an oxymoron. What we need today is something quite different: a critique of science that recognizes both its legitimacy and its limits.

Humanists who, citing Nietzsche out of context, would deconstruct the edifice of science only help render the humanities marginal in a world increasingly shaped by technology and science. Such humanists may well cite against me a provocative remark made by Richard Rorty in *Philosophy and the Mirror of Nature*. Today, Rorty claims, we can no longer say that Cardinal Bellarmine's objection to the Copernican theory, on the ground that it conflicted with the Scriptural description of the heavenly fabric, was illogical or unscientific.[38] According to Rorty, we do not know how to draw a clear line between theological and scientific discourse. This would open the door to a Christian science such as Bellarmine and Plantinga demand. I would like to counter with the opposite claim: if the humanities, and more especially philosophy, are not to become marginalized, they have to be able to explain just what it is that makes Cardinal Bellarmine's objections unscientific. The key to such an explanation is once again provided by the commitment to objectivity as a regulative ideal. That this remains an ideal must be accepted. But as such it is sufficient to give a direction. That non-scientific and, more especially, theological considerations have as a matter of fact played an important part in the history of science is no argument against this.

But if we are not to surrender freedom—and that means also humanity—to science, we must be able to show that reality may not be identified with the objects pursued by science. Just to be able to respond to a person as a person is to experience a reality that transcends what science can know, which is not to call science and its pursuit of the truth into question. But the very successes of science do raise a question, not for science, but for human beings concerned for their, and the world's, future. Just what room are we to give science in that world? Born of freedom, the successes of science and technology promise to finally make us masters and possessors of nature, including our own nature; promise thus an unheard-of freedom, but threaten at the same time to leave that freedom so empty that it will evaporate altogether. That loss of way in which philosophy has its origin remains very much with us.

And how could this not be so: some loss of way is inseparable from facing the future responsibly, that is to say, from freedom. The future is open. Different possibilities present themselves. And the more open the future, the more insistently the question "What should my place be?" will present itself.

I cited the story told by Socrates of the Thracian servant girl who laughed at Thales. The Athenians may similarly have laughed at Socrates. At least at first. They ended up condemning him to death for corrupting the young and believing in gods of his own invention instead of those recognized by the State. From their point of view the charges were quite justified: the freedom of philosophy is contagious, and the young are more likely than the old to be led by it to question what tradition has established; and although Socrates does invoke God and gods, he does not believe as his accusers do. To them the philosopher has to look like an atheist. But the freedom of Socrates remains bound—bound by a reality that calls him, that he serves and pursues, even though in the end all his conjectures about it remain inadequate. Despite all he has to teach, to the very end Socrates knows about his ignorance. And only such learned ignorance sustains philosophy.

Notes

1. Harry Frankfurt, "Concluding Discussion," in *Martin Heidegger: Politics, Art, and Technology,* ed. Karsten Harries and Christoph Jamme (New York: Holmes and Meier, 1994), 258.

2. Gotthold E. Lessing, "Eine Duplik," in his *Werke,* 10:53; quoted in Søren Kierkegaard, *Concluding Unscientific Postscript,* trans. David F. Swenson and Walter Lowrie (Princeton: Princeton University Press, 1968), 97.

3. Gaston Bachelard, *The Poetics of Space,* trans. Maria Jolas (Boston: Beacon, 1958), 61.

4. Friedrich Nietzsche, *The Birth of Tragedy,* §15, in *The Birth of Tragedy and the Case of Wagner,* trans. Walter Kaufmann (New York: Vintage, 1967), 95.

5. Richard Rorty, "Concluding Discussion," in *Martin Heidegger: Politics, Art, and Technology,* 259.

6. Ibid.

7. Nicholas Rescher, "American Philosophy Today," *Review of Metaphysics* 46 (4), 721.

8. Ibid., 722–723.

9. Arthur Danto, *Embodied Meaning* (New York: Farrar, Straus & Giroux, 1994), 312.

10. Rescher, "American Philosophy Today," 740.

11. Ibid., 719.

12. Ibid., 717.

13. Ibid., 723.

14. Karl-Otto Apel, *Transformation der Philosophie,* vol. 1 (Frankfurt am Main: Suhrkamp, 1976), 11.

15. Martin Heidegger, letter to Karl Jaspers of August 12, 1949 in *Martin Heidegger, Karl Jaspers—Briefwechsel* (Frankfurt am Main: Klostermann and Piper, 1990), xx. See Karsten Harries, "Shame, Guilt, Responsibility," in *Essays on Jaspers and Heidegger,* ed. Alan M. Olson (Philadelphia: Temple University Press, 1994), 49–64.

16. Rescher, "American Philosophy Today," 740.

17. Ibid., 727.

18. Ibid., 721.

19. Ibid., 723.

20. Ibid., 729.

21. Arthur Schopenhauer, preface to the second edition of *The World as Will and Representation,* vol. 1, trans. E. F. J. Payne (New York: Dover, 1969), xx.

22. Rescher, "American Philosophy Today," 733.

23. Ibid., 727.

24. Ibid., 734–735.

25. Richard Rorty, "Another Possible World," in *Martin Heidegger: Politics, Art, and Technology,* 35.

26. The question was raised by Reiner Schürmann. See "Concluding Discussion," in *Martin Heidegger: Politics, Art, and Technology,* 250.

27. Martin Heidegger, "Davoser Disputation," in *Kant und das Problem der Metaphysik, Gesamtausgabe,* vol. 3 (Frankfurt am Main: Klostermann, 1991), 286.

28. See Denis Hollier, *Against Architecture: The Writings of Georges Bataille,* trans. Betsy Wing (Cambridge: MIT Press, 1989).

29. Fyodor Dostoevsky, "Notes from the Underground," in *The Best Short Stories of Dostoevsky,* trans. David Margashack (New York: Modern Library, 1955), 139.

30. Ludwig Wittgenstein, *Philosophical Investigations,* trans. G. E. M. Anscombe (New York: Macmillan, 1953), §123.

31. Aristotle, *Metaphysics* I, 2, 982b, trans. W. D. Ross.

Karsten Harries

32. Plato, *Theaetetus* 1973, trans. E. B. Jowett.

33. Aristotle, *Metaphysics* I, 2, 982b.

34. Immanuel Kant, *Foundations of the Metaphysics of Morals,* trans. Lewis White Beck (Indianapolis: The Library of Liberal Arts, 1959), 52.

35. Cf. Paul Friedländer, "Aletheia," in *Plato,* vol. 1: *Introduction,* trans. Hans Meyerhoff (Princeton: Princeton University Press, Bollingen Series 59, 1969), 221–229.

36. Alvin Plantinga, "Methodological Naturalism?" *Origins & Design,* Winter 1997, 25.

37. Cited ibid.

38. Richard Rorty, *Philosophy and the Mirror of Nature* (Princeton: Princeton University Press, 1979), 328.

3

Reason, Expression, and the Philosophic Enterprise

Robert Brandom

We might begin by acknowledging a distinction between things that have *natures* and things that have *histories*. Physical things such as electrons and aromatic compounds would be paradigmatic of the first class, while cultural formations such as English Romantic poetry and Ponzi schemes would be paradigmatic of the second. Applied to the case at hand, this distinction would surely place philosophy on the side of things that have histories. But now we might ask: Does philosophy differ in this respect from physics, chemistry, or biology? Physical, chemical, and biological *things* have natures rather than histories, but what about the disciplines that define and study them? Should physics itself be thought of as something that has a nature or as something that has a history? Concluding the latter is giving a certain kind of pride of place to the historical. For it is in effect treating the *distinction* between things that have natures and things that have histories —between things studied by the *Naturwissenschaften* and things studied by the *Geisteswissenschaften*—as itself a cultural formation:

the sort of thing that itself has a history rather than a nature. And from here it is a short step (though not, to be sure, an obligatory one) to the thought that natures themselves are the sort of thing that have a history; certainly the *concepts* "electron" and "aromatic compound" are that sort of thing. At this point the door is opened to a thoroughgoing historicism. It is often thought that this is the point to which Hegel—one of my particular heroes—brought us. I think that thought is correct, as far as it goes, but that we go very wrong if we think that is where Hegel left us.

If philosophy is to be understood (at least to begin with) as the sort of thing that has a history rather than a nature, then our criteria for recognizing distinctively philosophical activity must answer to what precedential, tradition-transforming philosophers have actually done. One of Hegel's deepest and most important insights, I think, is that the determinate contentfulness of any universal—in this case, the concept of philosophy—can be understood only in terms of the process by which it incorporates the contingencies of the particulars to which it has actually been applied. But he goes on from there to insist that those of us who are heirs to such a conceptual tradition must ensure that it is a *rational* tradition—that the distinction it embodies and enforces between correct and incorrect applications of a concept can *be justified,* that applying it in one case and withholding application in another is something for which we can give *reasons.* Only insofar as we can do that are we entitled to understand what we are doing as applying *concepts.* We fulfill our obligation by rationally reconstructing the tradition: by finding a coherent, cumulative trajectory through it that reveals it as expressively progressive, as the gradual unfolding into greater explicitness of commitments that can be seen retrospectively as always already having been implicit in it. In other words, it is our job to rewrite the history so as to discover in it the revelation of what then retrospectively appears as an antecedent nature. Hegel balances the insight

Reason, Expression, Philosophic Enterprise

that even natures have histories by insisting that rationality itself requires us to construe histories as revelatory of natures.

The aim is to pick out, like a judge at common law, a sequence of precedential instances or applications of a concept which delineate that concept's content. *Making* the tradition rational is not independent of the labor of concretely *taking* it to be so. To be adequate, each such Whiggish rewriting of our disciplinary history must create and display continuity and progress by its systematic inclusions and exclusions. The discontinuities that correspond to shifts of topic, the forgetting of lessons, and the degeneration of research programs are invisible from within each such telling; but those differences live on in the spaces between the tellings. Each generation redefines its subject by offering a new retrospective reading of its characteristic concerns and hard-won lessons. But also, at any one time there will be diverse interpretations, complete with rival canons and competing designations of heroes and heroic feats. Making canons and baking traditions out of the rich ingredients bequeathed us by our discursive predecessors is a game that all can play. In this chapter, I will join the game by sketching one such perspective on what philosophers do. I will discern the nature of philosophy as it is revealed in history.

Ours is a broadly cognitive enterprise. By "broadly cognitive" I mean to indicate that philosophers aim at a kind of *understanding;* not, more narrowly, at a kind of *knowledge.* To specify the distinctive sort of understanding that is the characteristic goal of philosophers' writing is to say what distinguishes philosophers from other sorts of constructive seekers of understanding, such as novelists and scientific theorists. I want to do so by focusing not on the peculiar genre of nonfiction creative writing by which philosophical understanding is typically conveyed (though I think that subject is worthy of consideration), but rather on what is distinctive about the understanding itself: both its particular topic and its characteristic goal.

Robert Brandom

Philosophy is a self-reflexive enterprise: understanding is not only the *goal* of philosophical inquiry, but its *topic* as well. We are its topic, but it is us specifically as *understanding* creatures: *discursive* beings, makers and takers of *reasons,* seekers and speakers of *truth.* Seeing philosophy as addressing the nature and conditions of our rationality is, of course, a very traditional outlook—so traditional, indeed, that it is liable to seem quaint and old-fashioned. I'll address this issue later, remarking now only that rationalism is one thing, and intellectualism another: pragmatists, too, are concerned with the practices of giving and asking for reasons.

I understand the task of philosophers to have as a central element the explication of concepts—or, put slightly more carefully, the development and application of expressive tools with which to make explicit what is implicit in the use of concepts. When I say "explication of concepts," it is hard not to hear "analysis of meanings." There are obviously affinities between my specification and that which defined the concern of "analytic philosophy" in the middle years of the twentieth century. Indeed, I intend, *inter alia,* to be saying what was right about that conception. But what I have in mind is different in various ways. *Explication,* making explicit, is not the same as *analysis,* at least as that notion was classically conceived. As I use the term, for instance, we have no more privileged access to the contents of our concepts than we do to the facts we use them to state; the concepts and the facts are two sides of one coin.

But the most important difference is that where analysis of meanings is a fundamentally *conservative* enterprise (consider the paradox of analysis), I see the point of explicating concepts to be opening them up to rational *criticism.* The rational enterprise, the practice of giving and asking for reasons that lies at the heart of discursive activity, requires not only criticizing *beliefs* as false or unwarranted, but also criticizing *concepts.* Defective concepts distort our thought and constrain us by limiting the propositions and

Reason, Expression, Philosophic Enterprise

plans we can entertain as candidates for endorsement in belief and intention. This constraint operates behind our backs, out of our sight, since it limits what we are so much as capable of being aware of. Philosophy, in developing and applying tools for the rational criticism of concepts, seeks to free us from these fetters, by bringing the distorting influences out into the light of conscious day, exposing the commitments implicit in our concepts as vulnerable to rational challenge and debate.

"Concept" is a *normative* concept. This is a lesson we owe ultimately to Kant—the great, gray mother of us all. Kant saw us above all as traffickers in concepts. In fact, in a strict sense, *all* that Kantian rational creatures can do is to apply concepts. For that is the genus he took to comprise both *judgment* and *action,* our theoretical activity and our practical activity. One of Kant's great innovations was his view that what in the first instance distinguishes judgments and actions from the mere behavior of denizens of the realm of nature is that they are things that we are in a distinctive sense *responsible* for. They express *commitments* of ours. For Kant, concepts are the norms or rules that determine what we have committed ourselves to, what we have made ourselves responsible for in making a judgment or performing an action. Judging and acting involves undertaking commitments whose credentials are always potentially at issue. That is, the commitments embodied in judgments and actions are ones we may or may not be *entitled* to, so that the question of whether they are *correct,* whether they are commitments we *ought* to acknowledge and embrace, can always be raised. One of the forms taken by the responsibility we undertake in judging and acting is the responsibility to give reasons that justify the judgment or the action. And the rules—the concepts we apply in judging and acting—determine what would count as a reason for the judgment and the action.

Commitment, entitlement, responsibility—these are all normative notions. Kant replaces the *ontological* distinction between the physical and the mental with the *deontological* distinction between the realm of nature and the realm of freedom: the distinction between things that merely act regularly and things that are subject to distinctively normative sorts of assessment. Thus for Kant the great philosophical questions are questions about the source and nature of normativity—of the bindingness or validity (*Gultigkeit*) of conceptual rules.

Descartes had bequeathed to his successors a concern for *certainty:* a matter of our grip on concepts and ideas—paradigmatically, whether we have a hold on them that is clear and distinct. Kant bequeaths to his successors a concern rather for *necessity:* a matter of the grip concepts have on us, the way they bind or oblige us. "Necessary" (*notwendig*) for Kant just means "according to a rule" (that is why he is willing to speak of moral and natural necessity as species of a genus). The important lesson he takes Hume to have taught isn't about the threat of skepticism, but about how empirical knowledge is unintelligible if we insist on merely describing how things in fact are, without moving beyond that to prescribing how they *must* be, according to causal rules, and how empirical motivation (and so agency) is unintelligible if we stay at the level of "is" and eschew reference to the *ought's* that outrun what merely is. Looking further back, Kant finds "the celebrated Mr. Locke" sidetracked into a mere "physiology of the understanding"—the tracing of causal antecedents of thought in place of its justificatory antecedents—through a failure to appreciate the essentially normative character of claims to knowledge. But Kant takes the whole Enlightenment to be animated by an at least implicit appreciation of this point. For humanity's coming into its intellectual and spiritual majority and maturity consists precisely in taking the sort of personal responsibility for its commitments, both doxastic and practical, insisted upon already by Descartes's meditator.

This placing of normativity at the center of philosophical concern is the reason behind another of Kant's signal innovations: the pride of place he accords to *judgment*. In a sharp break with tradition, he takes it that the smallest unit of experience, and hence of awareness, is the judgment. This is because judgments, applications of concepts, are the smallest unit for which knowers can be *responsible*. Concepts by themselves don't express commitments; they only determine what commitments would be undertaken if they were applied (Frege expresses this Kantian point by saying that judgeable contents are the smallest unit to which pragmatic force—paradigmatically the assertional force that consists in the assertor undertaking a special kind of commitment—can attach. Wittgenstein distinguishes sentences from terms and predicates as the smallest expressions whose freestanding utterance can be used to make a move in a language game). The most general features of Kant's understanding of the form of judgment also derive from its role as a unit of responsibility. The "I think" that can accompany all representations (hence being, in its formality, the emptiest of all) is the formal shadow of the transcendental unity of apperception, the locus of responsibility determining a co-responsibility class of concept-applications (including actions), what is responsible for its judgments. The objective correlate of this subjective aspect of the form of judgment is the "object = X" to which the judgment is directed, the formal shadow of what the judgment makes the knower responsible to.

I think that philosophy is the study of us as creatures who judge and act—that is, as discursive, concept-using creatures. And I think that Kant is right to emphasize that understanding what we do in these terms is attributing to us various kinds of normative status, taking us to be subject to distinctive sorts of normative appraisal. So a central philosophical task is understanding this fundamental normative dimension within which we dwell. Kant's own approach to this issue, developing themes from Rousseau, is based on the thought that genuinely normative authority (constraint by norms) is distinguished from causal power (constraint by facts) in that it binds only those who *acknowledge* it as binding. Because one is subject only to that authority one subjects oneself to, the normative realm can be understood equally as the realm *of freedom*. So being constrained by norms is not only compatible with freedom—properly understood, it can be seen to be what freedom consists in. I don't know of a thought that is deeper, more difficult, or more important than this.

Kant's most basic idea, I said, is that judgment and action are things we are in a distinctive way *responsible* for. What does it mean to be responsible for them? I think the kind of responsibility in question should be understood to be task responsibility: the responsibility to do something. What (else) do judging and acting oblige us to do? The commitments we undertake by applying concepts in particular circumstances—by judging and acting—are ones we may or may not be entitled to, according to the rules (norms) implicit in those concepts. Showing that we are entitled by the rules to apply the concept in a particular case is *justifying* the commitment we undertake thereby, offering *reasons* for it. That is what we are responsible for, the practical content of our conceptual commitments. In undertaking a conceptual commitment, one renders oneself in principle liable to demands for reasons. The normative appraisal to which we subject ourselves in judging and acting is appraisal of our reasons. Further, offering a reason for the application of a concept is always applying another concept: making or rehearsing another judgment or undertaking or acknowledging another practical commitment (Kant's "adopting a maxim"). Conceptual commitments both serve as and stand in need of reasons. The normative realm inhabited by creatures who can judge and act is not only the realm of freedom, it is the realm of reason.

Understanding the norms for correct application that are implicit in concepts requires understanding the role those concepts play in reasoning: what (applications of concepts) count as reasons for the application of that concept, and what (applications of concepts) the application of that concept counts as a reason for. For apart from such understanding, one cannot fulfill the responsibility one undertakes by making a judgment or performing an action. So what distinguishes concept-using creatures from others is that we know our way around the *space of reasons*. Grasping or understanding a concept is simply being able practically to place it in a network of inferential relations: to know what is evidence for or against its being properly applied to a particular case, and what its proper applicability to a particular case counts as evidence for or against. Our capacity to know (or believe) *that* something is the case depends on our having a certain kind of know-how: the ability to tell what is a reason for what.

The cost of losing sight of this point is to assimilate genuinely conceptual activity, judging and acting, too closely to the behavior of mere animals—creatures who do not live and move and have their being in the normative realm of freedom and reason. We share with other animals (and for that matter, with bits of automatic machinery) the capacity reliably to respond differentially to various kinds of stimuli. We, like they, can be understood as classifying stimuli as being of certain kinds, insofar as we are disposed to produce different repeatable sorts of responses to those stimuli. We can respond differentially to red things by uttering the noise "That is red." A parrot could be trained to do this, as pigeons are trained to peck at one button when shown a red figure and another when shown a green figure. The empiricist tradition is right to emphasize that our capacity to have empirical knowledge begins with and crucially depends on such reliable differential responsive dispositions. But though the story begins with this sort of classification, it does not end there. For the rationalist tradition is right to emphasize that our classificatory responses count as applications of concepts, and hence as candidates for knowledge, only by virtue of their role in reasoning. The crucial difference between the parrot's utterance of the noise "That is red" and the (let us suppose physically indistinguishable) utterance of a human reporter is that for the latter, but not the former, the utterance has the practical significance of making a claim. Making a claim is taking up a normative stance of a kind that can serve as a premise from which to draw conclusions. That is, it can serve as a reason for taking up other stances. And further, it is a stance that itself can stand in need of reasons, at least if challenged by the adoption of other, incompatible stances. Where the parrot is merely responsively sounding off, the human counts as applying a concept just insofar as she is understood as making a move in a game of giving and asking for reasons.

The most basic point of Sellars's rationalist critique of empiricism in his masterwork *Empiricism and the Philosophy of Mind* is that even the non-inferentially elicited perceptual judgments that the empiricist rightly appreciates as forming the empirical basis for our knowledge can count as judgments (applications of concepts) only insofar as they are *inferentially* articulated.[1] Thus the idea that there could be an autonomous language game (a game one could play though one played no other) consisting entirely of non-inferentially elicited reports—whether of environing stimuli or of the present contents of one's own mind—is a radical mistake. To apply any concepts non-inferentially, one must be able also to apply concepts inferentially. For it is an essential feature of concepts that their applications can both serve as and stand in need of reasons. Making a report or a perceptual judgment is doing something that essentially, and not just accidentally, has the significance of making available a premise for reasoning. Learning to observe requires learning to infer. Experience and reasoning are two sides of one

coin, two capacities presupposed by concept use that are in principle intelligible only in terms of their relations to each other.

What distinguishes specifically conceptual classification from
classification merely by differential responsive disposition is the
inferential articulation of the response; applications of concepts are
essentially what can both serve as and stand in need of reasons.
Therefore, the game of giving and asking for reasons has a preeminent place among discursive practices. For what makes a practice
discursive in the first place is that it incorporates reason-giving
practices. Of course, there are many things one can do with concepts besides using them to argue and to justify. And it has seemed
perverse to some post-Enlightenment thinkers to privilege in any
way the rational, cognitive dimension of language use. But if the
tradition I have been sketching is right, the capacity to use concepts
in all the other ways explored and exploited by the artists and
writers whose imaginative enterprises have rightly been admired by
romantic opponents of logocentrism is parasitic on the prosaic inferential practices by virtue of which we are entitled to see concepts
as in play in the first place. The game of giving and asking for
reasons is not just one game among others one can play with language. It is the game by virtue of which what one has qualifies as
language (or thought) at all. Rationalism in this sense does not
entail intellectualism, the doctrine that every *implicit* mastery of a
propriety of practice is ultimately to be explained by appeal to a
prior *explicit* grasp of a principle. It is entirely compatible with the
sort of pragmatism that sees things the other way around.

As I am suggesting that we think of them, concepts are broadly
inferential norms that implicitly govern practices of giving and asking for reasons. Dummett has suggested a useful model for thinking
about the inferential articulation of conceptual contents.[2] Generaliz-
ing from the model of meaning Gentzen introduces for sentential
operators, Dummett suggests that we think of the use of any expres-

sion as involving two components: the circumstances in which it is appropriately used, and the appropriate consequences of such use. Because our concern is with the application of the concepts expressed by using linguistic expressions, we can render this as the circumstances of appropriate application of the concept, and the appropriate consequences of such application—that is, what follows from the concept's being applicable.

Some of the circumstances and consequences of applicability of a concept may be inferential in nature. For instance, one of the circumstances of appropriate application of the concept *red* is that this concept is applicable wherever the concept *scarlet* is applicable. And to say that is just another way of saying that the inference from "X is scarlet" to "X is red" is a good one. Similarly, one of the consequences of the applicability of the concept *red* is the applicability of the concept *colored*. And to say that is just another way of saying that the inference from "X is red" to "X is colored" is a good one. But concepts like *red* also have non-inferential circumstances of applicability, such as the visible presence of red things. Similarly, concepts such as *unjust* have non-inferential consequences of application—that is, they can make it appropriate to *do* (or not do) something, to *make* another claim true, not just to *say* or judge that it is true.

Even the immediately empirical concepts of *observables*, which have non-inferential *circumstances* of application and the immediately practical *evaluative* concepts, which have non-inferential *consequences* of application, however, can be understood to have contents that are inferentially articulated. For all concepts incorporate an implicit commitment to the propriety of the inference from their circumstances to their consequences of application. One cannot use the concept *red* as including the circumstances and consequences mentioned above without committing oneself to the correctness of the inference from "X is scarlet" to "X is colored." So we might decompose the norms that govern the use of concepts into three components: circumstances of appropriate application, appropriate consequences of application, and the propriety of an inference from the circumstances to the consequences. I would prefer to understand the inferential commitment expansively, as including the circumstances and consequences it relates, and so as comprising all three normative elements.

I suggested at the outset that we think of philosophy as charged with producing and deploying tools for the criticism of concepts. The key point here is that concepts may incorporate defective inferences. Dummett offers this suggestive example: the pejorative term *Boche*. The conditions for applying the term to someone is that he is of German nationality; the consequences of its application are that he is barbarous and more prone to cruelty than are other Europeans. We should envisage the connections in both directions as sufficiently tight as to be involved in the very meaning of the word: neither could be severed without altering its meaning. Someone who rejects the word does so because he does not want to permit a transition from the grounds for applying the term to the consequences of doing so. (It is useful to focus on a French epithet from the First World War, because we are sufficiently removed from its practical effect to be able to get a theoretical grip on how it works. But the thought should go over *mutatis mutandis* for pejoratives in current circulation.) Dummett's idea is that if you do not accept as correct the inference from German nationality to an unusual disposition to barbarity and cruelty, you can only reject the word. You cannot deny that there are any Boche, for that is just denying that the circumstances of application are ever satisfied, that is, that there are any Germans. And you cannot admit that there are Boche but deny that they are disposed to barbarity and cruelty (this is the "Some of my best friends are Boche" ploy), because that is taking back in one breath what one has asserted just before. Any use of the term commits the user to the inference that is curled up, implicitly, in it. At Oscar Wilde's trial the prosecutor read out some passages from *The Importance of Being Earnest* and said "I put it to you, Mr. Wilde, that this is blasphemy. Is it? Yes or no?" Wilde replied just as he ought on the account I am urging: "Sir, 'blasphemy' is not one of my words."[3]

Although they are perhaps among the most dangerous, highly charged words—words that couple "descriptive" circumstances of application with "evaluative" consequences of application—they are not alone in incorporating inferences we may need to criticize. The use of *any* expression involves commitment to the propriety of the inference from its circumstances to its consequences of application. These are almost never logically valid inferences. On the contrary, they are what Sellars called "material" inferences: inferences that articulate the content of the concept expressed. Classical disputes about the nature of personal identity, for instance, can be understood as taking the form of arguments about the propriety of such a material inference. We can agree, we may suppose, about the more or less forensic consequences of application of the concept "same person," having in mind its significance for attributions of (co-)responsibility. When we disagree about the circumstances of application that should be paired with it—for instance, whether bodily or neural continuity or the psychological continuity of memory counts for more—we are really disagreeing about the correctness of the inference from the obtaining of these conditions to the ascription of responsibility. The question about what is the correct concept is a question about which inferences to endorse. It is helpful to think about a great number of the questions we ask about other important concepts in these same terms: as having the form of queries about what inferences from circumstances to consequences of application we ought to acknowledge as correct, and why. Think in these terms about such very abstract concepts as *morally wrong, lust, beautiful, true, explain, know,* or *prove,* and again about "thicker" ones such as *unkind, cruel, elegant, just,* and *understand.*

The use of any of these concepts involves a material inferential commitment: commitment to the propriety of a substantial inferential move from the circumstances in which it is appropriate to apply the concept to the consequences of doing so. The concepts are substantive just because the inferences they incorporate are. Exactly this commitment becomes invisible, however, if one conceives conceptual content in terms of *truth conditions.* For the idea of truth conditions is the idea of a single set of conditions that are at once necessary and sufficient for the application of the concept. The idea of individually necessary conditions that are also jointly sufficient is the idea of a set of consequences of application that can also serve as circumstances of application. Thus the circumstances of application are understood as already including the consequences of application, so that no endorsement of a substantive inference is involved in using the concept. The idea of concepts like this is not incoherent. It is the ideal of *logical* or *formal* concepts. Thus it is a criterion of adequacy for introducing logical connectives that they be inferentially conservative: that their introduction and elimination rules be so related that they permit no new inferences involving only the old vocabulary. But it is a bad idea to take this model of the relation between circumstances and consequences of application of logical vocabulary and extend it to encompass also the substantively contentful nonlogical concepts that we use in most of our cognitive and practical transactions.

It is a bad idea because of its built-in conservatism. Understanding meaning or conceptual content in terms of truth conditions—individually necessary and jointly sufficient conditions—squeezes out of the picture the substantive inferential commitment implicit in the use of any nonlogical concept. But it is precisely those inferential commitments that are subject to *criticism* in the

Robert Brandom

light of substantive collateral beliefs. If one does not believe that Germans are distinctively barbarous or prone to cruelty, then one must not use the concept Boche, just *because* one does not endorse the substantive material inference it incorporates. On the other model, this diagnosis is not available. The most one can say is that one does not know how to specify truth conditions for the concept. But just what is objectionable about it, and why, does not appear from this theoretical perspective. Criticism of concepts is always criticism of the inferential connections. For criticizing whether all the individually sufficient conditions (circumstances) "go together," that is, are circumstances of application of one concept, is simply wondering whether they all have the same consequences of application (and similarly for wondering whether the consequences of application all "go together").

When we think of conceptual contents in the way I am recommending, we can see not only how beliefs can be used to criticize concepts, but also how concepts can be used to criticize beliefs. For it is the material inferences incorporated in our concepts that we use to elaborate the antecedents and consequences of various candidates for belief—to tell what we would be committing ourselves to, what would entitle us to those commitments, what would be incompatible with them, and so on. Once we accept that the inferential norms implicit in our concepts are in principle as revisable in the light of evidence as particular beliefs, conceptual and empirical authority appear as two sides of one coin. Rationally justifying our concepts depends on finding out about how things are: about what actually follows from what, as is most evident in the case of massively defective concepts such as Boche.

Adjusting our beliefs in light of the connections among them dictated by our concepts, and our concepts in light of our evidence for the substantive beliefs presupposed by the inferences they incorporate, is the rationally reflective enterprise introduced to us by

Socrates. It is what results when we consider the rational, normative connections among claims—connections that govern the practice of giving and asking for reasons—as themselves liable to demands for reasons and justification. Saying or thinking something, making it explicit, consists in applying concepts, thereby taking up a stance in the space of reasons, making a move in the game of giving and asking for reasons. The structure of that space, of that game, though, is not given in advance of our finding out how things are with what we are talking about—for what is *really* a reason for what depends on how things *actually* are. But that inferential structure itself can be the subject of claims and thoughts. It can itself be made explicit in the form of claims about what follows from what, what claims are evidence for or against what other claims, what else one would be committing oneself to by making a certain judgment or performing a certain action. So long as the commitment to the propriety of the inference from German nationality to barbarity and unusual cruelty remains merely implicit in the use of a term such as *Boche,* it is hidden from rational scrutiny. When it is made explicit in the form of the conditional claim "Anyone who is German is barbarous and unusually prone to cruelty," it is subject to rational challenge and assessment; it can, for instance, be confronted with such counterexamples as Bach and Goethe.

Discursive explicitness, the application of concepts, is Kantian apperception or consciousness. Bringing into discursive explicitness the inferentially articulated conceptual norms by virtue of which we can be conscious or discursively aware of anything at all is the task of reflection, or self-consciousness. This is the expressive task distinctive to philosophy. Of course, the practitioners of special disciplines, such as membrane physiology, are also concerned to unpack and criticize the inferential commitments implicit in using concepts such as *lipid soluble* (with a given set of circumstances and consequences of application). It is the emphasis on the "anything at all" which distinguishes philosophical reflection from the more focused reflection that goes on within such special disciplines. Earlier I pinned on Kant a view that identifies us as distinctively *rational* creatures, where that is understood as a matter of our being subject to a certain kind of *normative* assessment: we are creatures who can undertake *commitments* and *responsibilities* that are *conceptually* articulated in that their contents are articulated by what would count as *reasons* for them (as well as what other commitments and responsibilities they provide reasons for). One of philosophy's defining obligations is to supply and deploy an expressive toolbox, filled with concepts that help us make explicit various aspects of *rationality* and *normativity* in general. *The topic of philosophy is normativity in all its guises, and inference in all its forms.* And its task is an *expressive, explicative* one. So it is the job of practitioners of the various philosophical sub-fields to design and produce specialized expressive tools, and to hone and shape them with use. At the most general level, *inferential* connections are made explicit by *conditionals,* and their *normative* force is made explicit by *deontic* vocabulary. Different branches of philosophy can be distinguished by the different sorts of inference and normativity they address and explicate, the various special senses of "if . . . then" or of "ought" for which they care. Thus philosophers of science, for instance, develop and deploy conditionals codifying causal, functional, teleological, and other explanatory inferential relations, value theorists sharpen our appreciation of the significance of the differences in the endorsements expressed by prudential, legal, ethical, and aesthetic "ought's," and so on.

I said at the outset that I think of philosophy as defined by its history rather than by its nature, but that, following Hegel, I think our task of understanding consists in finding or making a nature in or from its history. The gesture I have made in that direction today, though, could also be summarized in a different kind of definition, namely in the ostensive definition: philosophy is the kind of thing that Kant and Hegel did (one might immediately want to add Plato, Aristotle, Frege, and Wittgenstein to the list, and then we are embarked on the enterprise of turning a gesture into a story, indeed, a history). So one might ask: Why not just say that, and be done with it? While, as I've indicated, I think that specification is a fine place to start, I also think there is a point to trying to be somewhat more explicit about just what sort of thing it is that Kant and Hegel (and Frege and Wittgenstein) did. Doing that is not being satisfied with a mere wave at philosophy as something that has a history. It is trying rationally to reconstruct that tradition, to recast it into a form in which we can see a constellation of ideas emerging, being expressed, refined, and developed.

With those giants, I see philosophy as a discipline whose distinctive concern is with a certain kind of *self-consciousness:* awareness of ourselves as specifically *discursive* (that is, concept-mongering) creatures. Philosophy's task is understanding the conditions, nature, and consequences of conceptual norms and the activities— starting with the social practices of giving and asking for reasons— that they make possible and that make them possible. As concept users, we are beings who can make explicit how things are and what we are doing (even if always only in relief against a background of implicit circumstances, conditions, skills, and practices). Among the things on which we can bring our explicating capacities to bear are those very concept-using capacities that make it possible to make anything at all explicit. Doing that, I am saying, is philosophizing.

It is easy to be misled by the homey familiarity of these sentiments, and correspondingly important to distinguish this characterization from some neighbors with which it is liable to be confused. There is a clear affinity between this view and Kant's coronation of philosophy as "queen of the sciences." For on this account philosophy does extend its view to encompass all activity that is discursive in a broad sense—that is, all activity that presupposes a capacity for judgment and agency, sapience in general. But in this sense, philosophy is at most *a* queen of the sciences, not *the* queen. For the magisterial sweep of its purview does not serve to distinguish it from, say, psychology, sociology, history, literary or cultural criticism, or even journalism. What distinguishes it is the *expressive* nature of its concern with discursiveness in general, rather than its inclusive scope. My sketch has aimed to introduce a specific difference pertaining to philosophy, not a unique privilege with respect to such other disciplines.

Again, as I have characterized it, philosophy does not play a *foundational* role with respect to other disciplines. Its claims do not stand prior to those of the special sciences in some order of ultimate justification. Nor does philosophy sit at the other end of the process as final judge over the propriety of judgments and actions—as though the warrant of ordinary theoretical and practical applications of concepts remained somehow provisional until certified by philosophical investigation. And philosophy as I have described it likewise asserts no methodological privilege or insight that potentially collides with the actual procedures of other disciplines.

Indeed, philosophy's own proper concerns with the nature of normativity in general—and with its conceptual species in particular, so with inference and justification in general—impinge on the other disciplines in a role that equally well deserves the characterization of "handmaiden." For what we do that has been misunderstood as having foundational or methodological significance is to provide and apply tools for unpacking the substantive commitments that are implicit in the concepts deployed throughout the culture, including the specialized disciplines of the high culture. Making those norms and inferences explicit in the form of claims exposes them for the first time to reasoned assessment, challenge, and defense, and so to the sort of rational emendation that is the primary process of conceptual evolution. But once the implicit presuppositions and consequences have been brought out into the daylight of explicitness, the process of assessment, emendation, and evolution is the business of those whose concepts they are, and not something philosophers have any particular authority over or expertise regarding. Put another way, it is the business of philosophers to figure out ways to increase semantic and discursive self-consciousness. What one does with that self-consciousness is not our business *qua* philosophers—though of course, *qua* intellectuals generally, it may well be.

Philosophy's *expressive* enterprise is grounded in its focus on us as a certain kind of thing, an expressing thing: as at once creatures and creators of conceptual norms, producers and consumers of reasons, beings distinguished by being subject to the peculiar normative force of the better reason. Its concern with us as specifically *normative* creatures sets philosophy off from the empirical disciplines, both the natural and the social sciences. It is this normative character that binds together the currents of thought epitomized in Stanley Cavell's characteristically trenchant aphorism that Kant de-psychologized epistemology, Frege de-psychologized logic, and Wittgenstein de-psychologized psychology. We might add that Hegel de-psychologized history. The de-psychologizing move in question is equally a de-sociologizing. For it is a refocusing on the *normative bindingness* of the concepts deployed in ground-level empirical knowledge, reasoning, and thought in general. This is a move beyond the narrowly *natural* (in the sense of the describable order of causes), toward what Hegel called the "spiritual" (*geistlich*), that is, the *normative* order.

That its concern is specifically with our *conceptual* normativity sets philosophy off from the other humanistic disciplines, from the literary as well as the plastic arts. We distinguish conceptual commitments by their inferential articulation, by the way they can serve

Robert Brandom

as reasons for one another, and by the way they stand in need of reasons, their entitlement always potentially being at issue. Now in asserting the centrality and indispensability, indeed, the criterial role, of practices of giving and asking for reasons, I am far from saying that reasoning—or even thinking—is all anyone ought to do. I am saying that philosophers' distinctive concern is, on the one hand, with what else those reason-mongering practices make possible, and how they do so; and on the other hand with what makes those practices possible: what sorts of doings count as sayings, how believing or saying that is founded on knowing how. This distinctive constellation of concerns makes philosophy the party of reasons, and philosophers the friends of the norms, the ones who bring out into the light of discursive explicitness our capacity to make things discursively explicit.

Notes

1. Wilfrid Sellars, *Empiricism and the Philosophy of Mind* (Cambridge: Harvard University Press, 1997).

2. Michael Dummett, *Frege: Philosophy of Language* (New York: Harper and Row, 1973), 454.

3. Of course, being right on this point didn't keep Wilde out of trouble, any more than it did Salman Rushdie.

4
Philosophy
Enlightenment Apology, Enlightenment Critique
Allen Wood

What is philosophy? If you ask a group of philosophy professors this question, there are several things you might hope to be told by way of an answer. You might want to hear how they think the subject of philosophy fits into an academic curriculum. You might want to watch them try to justify the place of philosophy, or of departments of philosophy, within a university. Or you might like to see different philosophers, representing different standpoints or specialties within the field, attempting to give an account of the field as a whole. You probably want to listen to them trying to vindicate their own philosophical positions or argue for the centrality (or at least the indispensability) of their own sub-field.

No doubt what I am going to say can be interpreted as a confession of why I have chosen to pursue an academic career in philosophy (I am sure these reasons will strike many as quixotic—they often strike me that way too). Also, because what I will say is shaped by the same things that account for my interests in ethics and in the history of modern philosophy, you will also hear something about those subjects. But I have to confess right at the start that in what follows I do not intend to meet any of the expectations I have just described. I will not argue directly for the importance of the history of philosophy or of philosophical theories about ethics or society. I am especially far from intending to explain or defend the existence of departments of philosophy within universities. Nor do I attach any importance to the question whether philosophy has a distinctive method or subject matter (for example, one dealing exclusively with a priori as distinct from empirical knowledge). I don't deny that reality is, and human knowledge should be, articulated and structured, and that knowledge may have distinguishable a priori and empirical components. Although philosophy is precisely the subject that discusses these issues, I do not think that they bear directly either on the question "What is philosophy?" or on whatever rationale there is for the existence of departments of philosophy within universities.

In my view, universities are not (and need not be) organized in ways that either "cut reality at the joints" or reflect the structure of human knowledge. Academic fields are (and should be) a function of the different traditions of research which have been successful in attracting and training members and in contributing something worthwhile to inquiry, scholarship, and pedagogy. The only rationale for the separate existence of any academic discipline or profession is that it has been, and is expected to continue to be, successful in this way. I think the academic field of philosophy more than meets that condition at present, but it won't be my aim here to defend this thesis.

Whatever else it may be, philosophy is a *self-reflective* activity, and therefore "What is philosophy?" is a *philosophical* question in a way that "What is poetry?" need not be the subject of poems (though of course it can be) and "What is physics?" is not a question for physicists (even if a knowledge of physics is needed in order to answer it). Because philosophy is a self-reflective activity with quite general scope, these other two questions actually belong to *philosophy,* along with questions like "What is truth?," "What is knowledge?," and "What is the good?"

Very few philosophers, however, spend much time trying to decide what philosophy is. I think they are quite correct in their relative neglect of "meta-philosophy." It even tells us something about philosophical reflection that "What is philosophy?" is *not* a fundamental (or even an especially important) philosophical question. Philosophical reflection gains its importance more from its discoveries about the objects of its reflection (about the nature of knowledge, goodness, beauty, and so forth) than from its own nature simply as philosophical reflection—discoveries which take the form of questions or perplexities as much as answers or assertable truths. Nor do we need to understand (or even to be perplexed by) the nature of philosophical reflection itself before we can begin making these discoveries. But I don't deny that philosophers can also ask "What is philosophy?," and they may learn something from this too.

Apologetic Questions and Analytical Questions

Questions of the form "What is *x?*"—where *x* is a human trait, faculty, function or activity of some kind—can always be asked in two ways. They can be asked either as *analytical* (that is, descriptive or explanatory) questions about what *x* in fact is, or else as normative or *apologetic* questions about what *x* should be. In the latter case, their answer tells us what *x* is only insofar as it is what it ought to be, and it is no objection to such an answer that the present state of *x* fails to correspond to this.

"What is Christianity?" asked by a committed Christian, and

"What is the American Way?" asked by a patriotic American, are usually framed as apologetic questions. Because in human life what exists is very seldom perfect—or to put it as Hegel would, because what exists contingently is never fully rational, hence never fully actual—to ask an *analytical* "What is *x*?" question about something human is often to invite an openly critical or even deflationary answer. No investigation of (really existing) Christianity can afford to ignore the roles moral hypocrisy and religious intolerance have played in this religion's practices, and no honest inquiry into the American Way can downplay the importance for American culture of such evils as white racism and capitalist exploitation. But for this very reason, apologetic treatments of Christianity will represent self-honesty and tolerance as among the Christian virtues, and an apologetic account of the American Way will include racial equality and liberty and justice for all.

In Book One of Plato's *Republic,* Thrasymachus is annoyed that Socrates and his friends consider the question "What is justice?" only apologetically, and proffers his own highly critical account of justice. In the *Gorgias,* Socrates himself more slyly treats the question "What is rhetoric?" in the same way, denying that rhetoric is a craft of persuasion aiming at the good of political power and claiming instead that it is merely a certain empirical knack for flattering and deceiving which does more harm than good to those who practice it.[1] There are philosophical views—which go back at least as far as Plato—according to which the right *analytical* account of anything is one which correctly identifies the thing's true nature and provides the right *apologetic* account of it. Thus to understand what justice is, Socrates and his friends in the *Republic* try to construct an image of the perfectly just state and the perfectly just soul. Likewise, he seeks to understand rhetoric in a deflationary way as a false appearance of justice, and then to seek an apologetic account of what justice is. Whether or not this is a correct account of the relation between the two questions about rhetoric and justice, both apologetic and critical questioning are legitimate, and they can supplement each other.

In asking "What is philosophy?" I am going to begin apologetically. My answer will not try to encompass everything that has gone by the name "philosophy." Nor will it try to sum up all possible apologetic accounts—which include many mutually conflicting ones. As with any apologetic account of anything, I will simply try to say what I think philosophy has been (albeit imperfectly) and what it most of all should go on being—hopefully, more perfectly.

One familiar story has it that philosophy began in ancient Greece with Thales of Miletus, who set out to use human intelligence, unmixed with poetic invention or religious myth, to investigate the nature of things. Whether this story contains historical truth or is itself only a myth of origins, it seems to me at least a myth conveying the right message. For I think an apologetic understanding of philosophy should stress its distinctness from both art and religion, and should focus on the attempt of unaided human reason to understand the world and act in it.[2]

Poetry, religion and philosophy are all forms of human thinking, and all seek in some way to define the ultimate ends of life, or at least to reflect on how or whether these can be defined. Poetic or artistic thinking does this in the course of making things (art objects) valued irrespective of their usefulness (for example, for their intrinsic perfection, or the intrinsic pleasantness of contemplating them or for some sort of special revelatory experience they afford). Poetic thinking may seek and find truth which is of interest to philosophy, just as philosophy may find truth that is useful in producing what is beautiful. But in art the revelation of truth is achieved not through rational thinking but through a direct intuition or perception. Religious thinking is often concerned with ultimate ends and with comprehending the whole of reality. But it seeks truth or ultimate ends through powers transcending the natural reasoning capacities of human beings. Philosophy does not necessarily spurn poetic inspiration or religious revelation—and it may even regard these as essential to achieving the ends of life—but it takes human reason to be the only permissible criterion of what is genuine in them, and in that sense to be their proper measure as well.

Philosophy and Enlightenment

My own favorite historical paradigm of philosophy is the eighteenth-century movement which called itself the "Enlightenment" (*éclaircissment, Aufklärung*). I will accordingly conceive my answer to the question "What is philosophy?" as an *Enlightenment* answer.

Kant defined *enlightenment* as the human being's emancipation from "self-incurred minority." Minority is a condition in which one's understanding is used only under the authority and direction of another, and minority is "self-incurred" when it is caused not by the immaturity or impairment of the understanding, but by its refusal to trust itself: it prefers the comfort and security of tutelage to the risks and responsibilities of thinking for oneself (Kant, 8:35).[3] The Enlightenment thought of itself as a philosophical age, and its best and most forward-looking thinkers proudly assumed the title of *philosophe*. They sought to make the independent, collective use of human reason into the final judge of all things—especially of human systems of thinking and of social institutions.

In some quarters there is skepticism about whether there was anything resembling a single project among eighteenth-century thinkers who thought of themselves as *lumières* or *Aufklärer*. In history, as in philosophy, there is always a great deal (too much, in fact) to be said on the skeptical side of every question. The sober-minded are always temperate in their consumption of skeptical arguments, as they are of all commodities that delight the palate of connoisseurs but are intoxicating and debilitating if enjoyed in excess. The best reason for viewing the Enlightenment as a real and a single movement is not that some Enlightenment philosophers saw themselves as part of such a movement; rather, it is that *we* ought to see ourselves as heirs of the Enlightenment, and therefore ought to include a unified understanding of the Enlightenment as an essential part of our self-understanding.

The enemies of Enlightenment, in the twentieth century as well as the eighteenth, often prominently include not only its natural enemies—political tyranny and religious superstition—but also some of its own offspring: those who see themselves (in contrast to what they criticize as Enlightenment's arrogant and false pretenses to intellectual and political emancipation) as the true freethinkers and liberators of the mind. One perniciously distorted view of the Enlightenment sees its essential traits as positivistic dogmatism, and the reduction of reason to instrumental reason—traits which in politics lead to a kind of scientistic statism in the service of whatever irrational goals happen to be lying at hand.[4] This in effect identifies Enlightenment exclusively with the deeds of its historic enemies and then criticizes it on the basis of values which the critics draw from nowhere but the Enlightenment itself. Where there is any truth at all in these criticisms—as when they reveal racist or patriarchal assumptions on the part of eighteenth-century philosophers—they merely blame the Enlightenment for not being already what precisely it has made us to be. Or even more unfairly, they blame it for not being already what we still aspire to be and are not.

The truth hidden in such charges is the acknowledgment that the Enlightenment tradition alone is the source of all these aspirations. But the charges themselves are often nothing but attempts to evade the responsibilities imposed by the acceptance of Enlightenment values. We see this in those who want to be always on the enlightened side of any moral or political issue but who also want to adopt a lightheartedly nihilistic attitude toward Enlightenment principles—as though their being on the right side were due merely to their own innate goodness, requiring no rational thought on their part. Critics of Enlightenment have always attacked it for being arrogant, hypocritical, and self-deceptive; but the worst forms of self-conceit and bad faith are surely to be found among these critics of it.

My contrast of philosophy with art and religion may remind some of Hegel's triadic division of the sphere of absolute spirit. But let us refine and correct such an account by looking for a moment at what the *philosophes* themselves thought about this question. In his preliminary discourse to the *Encyclopedia* (published in seventeen volumes between 1751 and 1765), Jean le Rond d'Alembert divides the works of the human mind into three spheres: (1) the sphere of *memory,* including history (both natural and human, sacred as well as profane) and all useful arts; (2) the sphere of *imagination,* which includes all "poetry" in the broadest sense, both sacred and profane, narrative, drama, painting, sculpture, and music; and (3) the sphere of *reason,* whose province is *philosophy.* This includes first *metaphysics* (the science of being in general, theology, and the knowledge of soul or spirit), second the knowledge of nature (which is divided into mathematics and physics), and third the knowledge of the human (which comprises logic and ethics) (*Discours preliminaire,* I:xlvii–lii, especially the table at l–li/144–145).[5]

In our day, on the other hand, philosophy is often contrasted with science—whether natural or social science. But as the *philosophes* understood philosophy, and as I intend to understand it, science is not fundamentally different from philosophy, but rather is one form philosophy can take. It was not until sometime in the nineteenth century that people began using the word *science* to refer to something that was supposed to be distinct from philosophy.[6]

There is no "scientific method" which distinguishes science from philosophy, religion, pseudo-science, or anything else. Science can be distinguished from philosophy only in the same contingent way that all academic disciplines and departments are distinguished from one another. Using the term *philosophy* in the apologetic sense I intend, the sciences are simply *parts* of it.[7]

An Enlightenment Apology

Let us look at what is arguably the most authentic source for an Enlightenment attempt to answer the apologetic question about philosophy: the *Encyclopedia,* its article on "Philosophy" and especially its more famous article entitled "Philosopher" (*Philosophe*). Both articles appeared anonymously. The article "Philosopher" was an abbreviation (perhaps by Denis Diderot) of a well-known short essay entitled *Apology for philosophy,* which was first published in 1743. This essay was attributed by Voltaire to his friend, the grammarian César Chesnau Dumarsais (1676–1756), whose chief work was a treatise on tropes or rhetorical figures of speech.[8] (The attribution to Dumarsais is doubtful, but here I will bracket these doubts.[9]) The *Apology* was well known in the eighteenth century, but because it is not well known today, I will summarize it here.[10]

Dumarsais begins by rejecting the common opinion that a philosopher is anyone who leads a withdrawn and unobtrusive life, as long as he has read a little and gives the appearance of wisdom (*Philosophe,* XII:509/284). In beginning this way, he is also acknowledging a familiar complaint against philosophers: that they are so proud of having freed themselves from the prejudices of their religious upbringing that they have become unsociable, arrogantly looking down on their fellow human beings, whom they regard as foolish, slavish, and pusillanimous. Dumarsais undertakes to reply by describing the *true* philosopher, and *correctly* distinguishing between the philosopher and the ordinary person.

Ordinary or un-philosophical people, he says, act without knowing the causes of their actions, or even suspecting that such causes exist. The fundamental trait of philosophers is to seek such causes and then consciously to let themselves be moved by the causes that move them, so as to avoid being acted on by causes they choose not to move them (*Philosophe,* XII:509/284). This, he says, is the true meaning of *reason,* and of leading a rational life: "Reason is to a philosopher what grace is to a Christian"—namely, the principle impelling them to act (*Philosophe,* XII:509/284). "Other men are carried away by their passions; their actions are not preceded by reflection: they are men who walk in darkness. A philosopher, on the other hand, even in moments of passion, acts only according to reflection: he walks through the night, but he is preceded by a torch" (*Philosophe,* XII:509/285).

Rational or free action involves no exemption from having one's actions caused, and no absence of passion. It does not even involve any exemption from the universal human condition of walking in darkness. Through the darkness, however, philosophers walk with a torch of self-knowledge. By becoming aware of the causes that move them, they acquire the critical capacity of selecting which causes (which thoughts, conditions, sentiments, and passions) these will be. Philosophers, therefore, accept no principle at face value but seek the *origins* of their principles, so that they may take every maxim from its source, knowing thereby both its true worth and the limits of its applicability (*Philosophe,* XII:509/285).[11] The philosopher accepts not only the true as true and the false as false, but also the probable and the doubtful for what they are. In other words, to be free or rational, to select which causes will move me by knowing the origin, worth, and scope of my maxims, I must always apportion belief precisely to the evidence. This contrasts with the practice of religious enthusiasts, whose love of truth has taken the corrupt form of a passionate will to believe. Since they cannot precisely confine the causes of their belief to the evidence for it, their belief must always remain in some way opaque and mysterious to them—a deficiency they disguise as an advantage when they ascribe their belief to divine inspiration (now we begin to understand Dumarsais's cryptic epigram: "Reason is to the philosopher what grace is to the Christian").

The article "Philosophy" tells us that the two greatest obstacles to philosophy are (1) authority, and (2) the systematic spirit (*Philosophie,* XII:514). The latter spirit of system actually nurtures the search for truth insofar as it encourages us to find connections between truths, but undermines the philosophic spirit when it leads us to see only what confirms our opinions and to ignore the arguments against them (*Philosophie,* XII:515). Authority, however, is the unconditional enemy of philosophy because (as with Kant's "self-incurred minority") it leads us to abdicate responsibility for our own thoughts by putting someone else's understanding in the place of our own. "A true philosopher does not see by the eyes of others and forms his own convictions only by the evidence" (*Philosophie,* XII:514).

It is not reliance on one's own reason, Dumarsais goes on to point out, that constitutes the worst and most dangerous form of intellectual pride and arrogance. It is rather the compulsive need to judge, the thought that it is shameful not to arrive at a decision and terrible to find oneself in a state of doubt (*Philosophe,* XII:510/285). "A philosopher is not so attached to a system as to be unable to understand the strength of the objections that can be raised against it. The majority of men are so strongly committed to their opinions that they do not even take the trouble to inquire into the opinions of others. The philosopher understands the point of view he rejects as clearly and to the same extent as his own" (*Philosophe,* XII:510/286).

Allen Wood

This leads into Dumarsais's response to the common accusation that the philosopher is isolated and unsociable. "Man is not a monster who should live only in the depths of the sea or the furthest reaches of the forest. . . . In whatever condition he finds himself, his needs and the desire for well-being oblige him to live in society. Reason demands that he know and study the qualities of sociability and endeavor to acquire them." In social life, therefore, "our philosopher does not believe he lives in exile; he does not believe himself to be in enemy territory" (*Philosophe*, XII:510/286). On the contrary, "he loves society profoundly." "He looks on civil society as a divinity on earth" (*Philosophe*, XII:510/287). Dumarsais thus urges that the true philosopher will necessarily be upright, a model of dutifulness and probity, the truest example of the *honnête homme* (*Philosophe*, XII:510/287). For the same reason, however, the true philosopher will be "far removed from the impassive sage of the Stoics": "The philosopher is a man, while their sage was only a phantom" (*Philosophe*, XII:510/288–289). "This love of society which is so essential in the philosopher proves the truth of the remark made by the Emperor Antonius: 'How happy will the peoples be when kings will be philosophers, or philosophers kings!'" (*Philosophe*, XII:510/288). Dumarsais concludes his portrait by remarking that the true philosopher, who takes pride in the humanity he shares with other human beings, is neither tormented by ambition nor satisfied, like an ascetic, with the bare necessities; instead, he enjoys the comforts of life in that "modest superfluity which alone brings happiness" (*Philosophe*, XII:511/289).

Philosophical Reflection and Sociability

Because Dumarsais's *Encyclopedia* article is an apology not for an activity but for a certain kind of person, it does not appear to respond directly to the question "What is philosophy?" Dumarsais's defense of the philosopher even appears to agree with the accusers on one point which today few philosophers (or at least professors of philosophy) would accept, namely, that the philosopher differs in significant ways from ordinary people. In fact, Dumarsais's reply to the charge of arrogance even adopts a line which most of us must find not only implausible but even openly self-defeating. For in effect his claim is not that philosophers are not arrogant, but instead that their arrogance is justified, because the true philosopher really is wiser, freer, and more virtuous than is the ordinary person.

Yet it is common enough that enduring philosophical issues are hard to recognize because they assume a different outward appearance in different ages. One of the principal reasons for studying the history of philosophy carefully is that the differing interpretation of issues in different times is an important part of their identity through time. We may sometimes be blind even to a statement of our own position on an issue because in an unfamiliar historical context, that position may wear a mask which is not only unfamiliar but even repellent to us. The charge that philosophers are arrogant and unsociable is, I suggest, only the eighteenth-century version of the familiar charge that "Intellectuals are elitists." Of course such accusations are leveled not only at academic philosophers, but perhaps even more at progressive-minded social scientists, literary theorists, feminists, and even natural scientists insofar as they try to intervene in social and political debates on a progressive side—that is, one that seeks greater civil freedom, less economic oppression, and a more rational community between human beings (in eighteenth-century terms: on the side of liberty, equality, and fraternity). Now as then, attempts to understand the world rationally (especially the social world) and to agitate for changes in a progressive direction are regarded as at best idealistic exercises in irrelevancy with no hope of success. But often critical detachment is not only seen as useless, but also attacked as dangerously subversive of the social order (or, in a leftist version of the charge, of this or that social movement).

Dumarsais's apology for philosophy answers that a true philosopher must "combine a reflective and precise mind with the manners and qualities of a sociable man" (*Philosophe*, XII:511/288). It is this claim alone which enables him to defend the philosopher against the charge that rational reflectiveness is merely a form of arrogance which isolates the philosopher from society. Dumarsais does not deny that philosophy may loosen the grip of some of the values its accusers hold dear (in particular, religious values). His reply is that philosophy supports the only kind of sociability which we *ought* to want in ourselves and our fellow citizens. But the arguments for this claim lie just beneath the surface of Dumarsais's highly rhetorical discourse.

Perhaps the one closest to the surface is this: the foundation of the philosopher's rational reflectiveness is her commitment to self-knowledge for the sake of action. The philosopher wants to know the causes moving her so that she may estimate their value and choose to be moved by those worthy of this choice. One obvious result of reflective self-knowledge, however, is the discovery that as a human being the philosopher needs to live with other human beings, and that in order to fulfill their human nature philosophers cannot withdraw from society but must cultivate in themselves the right kind of sociability. This argument clearly needs to be filled out by a demonstration that the philosopher needs a sociability of probity and devotion to the common interest rather than one of self-interested manipulation and opportunistic exploitativeness. But Dumarsais seems to me, at any rate, to be on the right track.

There is a still deeper argument suggested by Dumarsais's apology. The philosopher acts freely and rationally because she understands the causes which move her and knows the true origin of the principles she follows. This knowledge liberates her because it enables her to estimate the true worth of her motives and her maxims, and thus to be moved only by causes that can withstand rational reflection. That reflection, as Dumarsais describes it, is grounded on an understanding of principles opposed to one's own, and of the arguments that may be offered in favor of such foreign principles. Dumarsais points out that in order to acquire this understanding, the philosopher must attend to the opinions of others and understand the grounds for them just as well as she does her own opinions and the arguments for them. It is impossible for her to do this if she withdraws from society in the arrogant conviction of her own superiority, and it is equally impossible if she refuses to regard others with respect, or takes an interest in their opinions only insofar as she thinks they will provide her with an opportunity to advance her own self-interest. The philosopher's fundamental attribute of free action based on reflective self-understanding thus requires both sociability and respect for others.

As I have already observed, today we are much less inclined than Dumarsais to defend philosophy by arguing for the superiority of the philosopher as a special kind of person who is set apart from ordinary people. The argument I have just given points toward such a conclusion, which was drawn explicitly by Kant. For him, the term *philosophy* refers to a *science of wisdom*. *Wisdom* means a knowledge of the final ends of action. To call oneself a "philosopher," then, is to claim (in Kant's words) "to be a master in the knowledge of wisdom, which says more than a modest man would claim; and philosophy, as well as wisdom, would itself always remain an ideal" (Kant 5:109). Kant does not object to an ideal portrait of the philosopher as long as it serves to humble rather than to congratulate those to whom the title is to be applied: "On the other hand, it would do no harm to discourage the self-conceit of someone who ventures on the title of philosopher if one holds before him, in the very definition, a standard of self-estimation which would very much lower his pretension" (Kant 5:108–109).

Philosophers, insofar as this term can refer to actual human beings, are never very different from other people. But we might nevertheless preserve the substance of Dumarsais's apology if we said not that philosophers differ from ordinary people, but rather that it is unfortunately far from usual in human life for people to act, whether individually or collectively, on the basis of a reflection on their principles which understands the origins of these principles and involves a true estimation of their worth. The eighteenth century, insofar as it was the century of Enlightenment, witnessed the birth of many modern attempts at theories which provide this kind of understanding—theories now associated with names such as Rousseau, Smith, Bentham, Hegel, Marx, and Freud. Such theories seek to comprehend human life and also to transform it—sometimes radically. Reason is a capacity to know the world, but chiefly it is a capacity to act in it, and because reason is also oriented toward society, its vocation above all is to transform the social order—actualizing the Enlightenment ideals of liberty, equality, and fraternity. In the eighteenth century, this took the form of the struggle of liberal constitutionalism and republicanism against traditional aristocracies of birth backed by religious hierarchy and superstition. In the nineteenth and twentieth centuries, it has chiefly taken the form of a struggle against forms of oppression based on economic class, race, culture, and gender.

An Enlightenment Critique of Philosophy

The Enlightenment tradition's record of success in these struggles has been mixed at best. Seen in this light, Dumarsais's portrait of the ideal philosopher as different from the ordinary person is an acknowledgment of the fact that the possibility of a life (above all, a collective social life) guided by rational reflection remains an ideal which stands in sharp contrast to the ordinary life in which we find ourselves enmeshed, for which what counts is not reason and self-transparent reflection, not free communication and public-spirited community, but only a system of collective unfreedom driven by the blind competition for power, wealth, and prestige, in which forms of communication increasingly take merely the form of tools or weapons which are ever more exclusively at the disposal of dominant powers.

These considerations point directly to the analytical (or critical) consideration of the question "What is philosophy?" I confess that this critique, which is required to complement my apologetic consideration of the question, has been delayed too long here, no doubt by my fondness for—or even partisanship toward—philosophy. Its starting point is Dumarsais's insight that critical reflection is from and for society, that philosophy arises out of our sociability and is meant to belong to it. Yet as *philosophy,* critical thinking appears as the individual possession of individuals—even of a few peculiar individuals (philosophers) who must defend themselves against the charge of being unsociable. Even when the Enlightenment grasped philosophy as a social activity of critical reflection, it understood it as an activity set apart from actual social life—an isolation that was meant to win toleration for it but that also made it seem artificial and impotent. For Kant and the German Enlightenment, the social side of philosophy was the province of *Gelehrten*—"scholars" or "the learned," people who are to be free to address one another in a public forum simply as rational individuals, members of a *learned public,* even if their actions and speech must also be restricted by their duties to the state and to their professions when they are considered as *private persons* (Kant 8:36–41). It was not difficult for Kant's counter-Enlightenment friend Hamann to satirize this conception, characterizing the "public use of reason" as merely a

Allen Wood

"sumptuous dessert" to be enjoyed only after the private use of reason supplies one's "daily bread."[12] Philosophy, then, is condemned to be a form of critical thinking which aims at practical transformation of the world but remains essentially divorced from that world. Philosophy succumbs to its own dialectic: to understand what it *is* is to understand why it can never be what it aims to be.

This critique of Enlightenment philosophy, like other more fashionable critiques of Enlightenment thinking, was already clearly understood by the Enlightenment itself. In the brilliant satirical dialogue *Rameau's Nephew,* Denis Diderot confronts the Enlightenment philosopher (ostensibly Diderot himself) with the dark, ironical reflections of an envious second-rate musician (who is, however, a first-rate wit and social sycophant). The nephew of the famous composer Rameau has just been ostracized from the world of the rich and powerful because, in an unguarded moment of excessive honesty, he has offended his social patron.[13] The younger Rameau represents the corrupt world the philosopher finds around him, yet he also sees its internal contradictions far more clearly than the philosopher does. Further, he sees the essential hollowness of philosophy, its uselessness and irrelevance to real life as it is being lived (*Rameau,* pp. 30–34, 62–66). The moralizing philosopher can only stand aloof from the entire social milieu Rameau so wittily and perceptively analyzes, condemning equally its hypocrisy and Rameau's irreverent, amoralistic critique of it. As for Rameau, himself, the philosopher has nothing to advise beyond acceptance of things as they are, and even tells Rameau he should make it up with those he has offended (*Rameau,* pp. 32, 40, 62).

No one can ever be sure what Diderot had in mind in writing *Rameau's Nephew.* But the lessons I think *we* should take away from it are that the social role of the philosopher in modern society is deeply problematic, and that Enlightenment philosophy's exclusively moralistic approach both to personal life and social reform is hopelessly shallow. The rational reflection that is supposed to constitute the foundation of the philosopher's life will always remain defective unless it includes a comprehension of social reality enabling it to understand the social role and function of philosophy itself and leading to a practical orientation toward that reality which actualizes the goals of reflective reason.

We can best put the critical point I am making about philosophy if we use the vocabulary of a later stage in the development of the Enlightenment tradition, and say that philosophy is essentially *ideology*. By this I mean what Marx meant: that it is thinking separated from social practice, which for this very reason can never achieve its own essential aim of self-transparent rational action. Philosophy is condemned either to endorse the existing social order by mystifying it, or else to stand over against that order as a critical reflection which comprehends and rejects it but has no power to change it. The early Marx stated this best when he said that it is for practice not to negate philosophy but to actualize it, but the actualization of philosophy is at the same time the *Aufhebung* of philosophy.[14] If we translate this out of the language of young Hegelianism into the more contemporary language I have been using, what it means is that critical reflection can direct action only if it ceases to play the kinds of social roles it has played in modern society thus far, and becomes instead an aspect of a social movement transforming society. "Philosophers have only *interpreted* the world differently, what matters is to *change* it."[15]

Of course Marx thought he knew just *how* philosophy was to be actualized. He offered the remarks just quoted as advice simultaneously to philosophers and to political activists. The proletariat was to find its intellectual weapons in philosophy, just as philosophy was to find its material weapons in the proletariat. The actualization (and simultaneous Aufhebung) of philosophy was to constitute the universal emancipation of humanity.[16] Unfortunately, I have no such knowledge, and do not mean my remarks as the sort of advice Marx thought he was in a position to give. Nor, apart from my reservations about the excessively moralistic emphasis of Enlightenment philosophy, do I mean to criticize the *kind of thinking* represented by philosophy as Dumarsais describes it—and by extension, as it is represented by the radical tradition of Enlightenment thought down to the present day. Both philosophy and society are unfortunately still at the stage where the world must be interpreted differently before it can be changed. My chief complaint about the radical Enlightenment tradition in this respect is only the obvious one—that its representatives seem to be too few, and their influence on the course of things is too weak.

I am especially far from agreeing with the fashionable criticisms of Enlightenment thought which say that "reason" is just another mode of power, and that the class of philosophers (or intellectuals), with its scientific pretensions, is merely another priesthood seeking to bring humanity under its tutelage. I reject these charges not because there is no truth in them but because they are in no way criticisms of Enlightenment *principles*. On the contrary, they presuppose not only those principles but even to a considerable extent the Enlightenment conception of society and history. In effect they accuse the enlighteners only of failing to fulfill their self-appointed historical vocation.

Foucault is certainly right when he describes the genuine accomplishment of the Enlightenment as "an ethos, a philosophical life in which the critique of what we are is at one and the same time the historical analysis of the limits that are imposed on us and an experiment with the possibility of going beyond them."[17] But we should *not* say (as Foucault does) that when people live in this spirit, they are merely *seeking* the mature adulthood of enlightenment. Rather, they have already achieved it, and their further search for the standpoint of reason is simply the human condition as it must be taken over by mature adults. The obstacle, now as in the eighteenth century, is simply that the world is ruled by enemies of this enlightened ethos, and hence those who share in it cannot integrate what Foucault here calls the "philosophical life" into their real lives. This in turn is because, as Diderot's dialogue already made dramatically clear, even the most enlightened individuals do not belong to a society whose practical life coheres even minimally with the demands of reflective reason.

It seems to me, however, that the real motivation behind the recently fashionable internal critiques of Enlightenment has often been nothing more than that the progressive causes spawned by the Enlightenment have *failed*—that they have either ceased to move forward or else (as in the case of Marxist socialism) are commonly thought to have met with final historic annihilation. The critics, who sympathize with the aims of the vanquished causes, are in a state of confusion because they cannot understand what went wrong, and since they lack the maturity Kant took to be the essence of Enlightenment, their first priority is to find a psychological defense against the humiliation of defeat. Their critiques of the Enlightenment are like the curses hurled at a charismatic leader by followers who trusted in his invincibility and now experience his downfall as an act of personal betrayal.

What the critics really want is a reconceptualization of progressive thinking and practice. But they have no clear idea of what they are seeking, nor will they ever get any as long as they sink themselves in skepticism, aestheticism, and self-subversion. They simply have yet to face up to the fact that the historic defeats are due not to internal flaws in Enlightenment but to the superior power, at least for the time being, of its traditional enemies—above all entrenched systems of power and privilege, which know very well how to deploy to their advantage the deadly charm of custom, the comfort of old superstitions, and infantile fears in the face of freedom.

Allen Wood

Those of us who continue to share the aims of philosophy as the Enlightenment conceived it cannot pursue these aims in any confident spirit of historical inevitability. Our spirit must instead be one of sober recognition that for an honest, thinking human being—a philosopher, in Dumarsais's sense—there is simply no acceptable alternative. This is why even such twentieth-century critics of Enlightenment as Adorno and Foucault do not, in the end, decisively break with it. Supporters of Enlightenment can sympathize with their search for new and less compromised ways to articulate its aims. And of course we, too, hunger for more effective strategies for realizing those aims under altered historical circumstances. But such new strategies are simply new devices for making the eighteenth-century ideals recognizable to a time in which they have been effaced, and for discovering (or creating) new agencies to play the familiar roles in a fundamentally unchanged narrative of human liberation.

Writing about the *Encyclopedia* in the *Encyclopedia,* Diderot proclaimed that it was "possible only as the endeavor of a philosophical century" (*Encyclopédie* V:644/18).[18] In an *un*philosophical century such as ours, the defense of philosophy can consist only in the reassertion of the most radical aims of the Enlightenment in a spirit of patient perseverance and (if need be) of stubborn impenitence.

Notes

1. Plato, *Republic* 343–348, *Gorgias* 463–465.

2. Perhaps it is not even possible to form the concept of philosophy, in the sense in which I mean the term, except in a context where the natural and self-directed use of our cognitive faculties can be distinguished from other uses, directed from outside by other forces, such as tradition, poetic inspiration, or religious revelation.

3. References to Kant are to volume number, then page number in

Kants Schriften, in the Akademie Ausgabe (Berlin: de Gruyter, 1900), except for references to the *Critique of Pure Reason,* which use A/B pagination.

4. See Michel Foucault, "What is critique?" in *What Is Enlightenment? Eighteenth-Century Answers and Twentieth-Century Questions,* ed. James Schmidt (Berkeley: University of California Press, 1996), 388. This portrayal, of course, is only a latter-day version of the famous diatribe in Horkheimer and Adorno, *The Dialectic of Enlightenment,* trans. John Cummig (New York: Continuum, 1973).

5. All citations from *Encyclopédie, ou Dictionnaire raisonné des sciences, des arts et des métiers, par une société des gens des lettres. Mis en ordre à publié par M. Diderot* (Paris: Briasson, 1751–1765) will be by French title of the article or essay followed by the volume and page numbers in the original edition. Where translations are also cited, the English edition is noted at the first occurrence and the page number(s) of the translation are given following the French page number(s), separated by a slash (/). Jean le Rond d'Alembert, "Discours Preliminaire," is cited in the following English translation: *Preliminary Discourse to the Encyclopedia of Diderot,* trans. R. Schwab (Indianapolis: Bobbs-Merrill, 1963).

6. The full title of Newton's *Principia* means "The Mathematical Principles of Natural Philosophy." In the first half of the nineteenth century, items of laboratory equipment were still referred to as "philosophical instruments." The terms *philosophy* and *philosophical,* in my view, are entirely appropriate in that title. "Scientific" thinking can be distinguished from philosophy only by the ways in which specific subject matters have been successfully dealt with through determinate investigative techniques, methods, and theories. The idea that there is something called "the scientific method" which says what the sciences have in common, and how they are distinct from philosophy or metaphysics, has always seemed to me a false idea.

7. Physics can be a part of philosophy without the philosophical question "What is physics?" being part of physics. This is because physics is not that part of philosophy whose business includes asking what physics is. The differences between philosophy and science could be thought of

Allen Wood

{ 118 }

metaphorically as generational ones, where philosophy could be thought of as a (middle-aged) parent and science is its (adolescent or young adult) child. According to a familiar stereotype, such children tend to be overconfident and a bit cocky, anxious to be independent of their parents, impatient with the parents' slowness to change, with their attachment to old ideas and reluctance to throw them over for new ones. The child sometimes rushes headlong into unwise enterprises against which the parent warns it. Sometimes these warnings are wise, but sometimes they show excessive caution and insufficient recognition of the fact that the world of the child is a new one, for which the parent's experience is no longer a secure guide. In a similar way, science sometimes sees no serious point in philosophical questions, thinking that it has found a way either to answer them (if they are worth answering) or else to avoid them (as not worth the trouble). Notoriously, some of the greatest scientific discoveries had to overcome resistance from philosophers who were reluctant to accept the fundamental changes in thinking these discoveries demanded of them. On the other hand, many theories trumpeted by their founders and proponents as "scientific"—whether they are theories within science or theories about science—have been propounded with great overconfidence, only to be utterly discredited a few generations later, outlived by the philosophical questions and doubts they treated with contempt. More important than the family squabbling between science and philosophy, however, is their intimate kinship and the fundamental continuity between them.

8. This essay is still of interest to literary theorists and has been republished. See Dumarsais, *Des tropes, ou, Des differents sens* (Paris: Flammarion, 1988).

9. The history and attribution of this essay is dealt with extensively in Herbert Dieckmann, *Le Philosophe* (St. Louis: Washington University Studies, New Series, No. 18, 1948). Dieckmann casts doubt both on the attribution of the essay to Dumarsais and on the idea that it was Diderot himself who adapted it for the *Encyclopedia*. English citation of the article "Philosopher" is to the following translation: Diderot, D'Alembert et al., *Encyclopedia (Selections)*, trans. N. Hoyt and T. Cassirer (Indianapolis: Bobbs-Merrill, 1965), 283–290.

10. The *Encyclopedia* version of the article omits some explicit attacks on religion included in the longer versions of Dumarsais's essay. There is also a book-length study purporting to contain Dumarsais's apology, but apparently written by d'Holbach. It is in Paul Henri Thiry, baron d'Holbach, *Essai sur les préjugés, ou, De l'influence des opinions sur les moeurs & sur le bonheur des hommes: Ouvrages contenant l'apologie de la philosophe par Dumarsais* (Paris: J. Desray, L'an I de la République français [1792]). Virtually no verbatim quotations from the *Apology* appear in this volume, however.

11. As Dumarsais puts it, to the philosopher, even truth is not like a "mistress who corrupts his imagination, and therefore appears to him everywhere" (*Philosophe,* XII:509/285).

12. J. G. Hamann, Letter to Christian Jacob Kraus, 18 December 1784, in Schmidt, *What Is Enlightenment?,* 148.

13. Denis Diderot, *Le neveu de Rameau/Rameaus Neffe,* Dual language (French-German) edition (Frankfurt: Insel, 1996). Abbreviated as "*Rameau,*" and cited by page number in the French version. The dialogue was composed sometime after 1761, but still published at Diderot's death in 1784, and remained unknown until 1805, when a copy of the manuscript (which was among Diderot's papers left at the court of Catherine the Great of Russia) apparently found its way to Schiller and was published in a German translation by Goethe.

14. Karl Marx, "Critique of Hegel's Philosophy of Right: Introduction" (1843), in *Marx: Selections,* ed. Allen Wood (New York: Macmillan, 1988), 28.

15. Ibid., 82.

16. Ibid., 33–34.

17. Michel Foucault, *A Foucault Reader,* ed. Paul Rabinow (New York: Pantheon, 1984), 50.

18. The English citation is to Denis Diderot, *Encyclopédie* in *The Portable Enlightenment Reader,* ed. Isaac Kramnick (New York: Penguin, 1995).

Allen Wood

5

Public Philosophy and International Feminism

Martha C. Nussbaum

Do you want to know what philosophy offers humanity? Practical guidance. One man is on the verge of death. Another is rubbed down by poverty. . . . These are ill treated by men, those by the gods. Why, then, do you write me these frivolities? There is no time for playing around: you have been retained as lawyer for unhappy humanity. You have promised to bring help to the shipwrecked, the imprisoned, the sick, the poor, to those whose heads are under the poised axe.

—Seneca, *Moral Epistles*

For from what is said truly but not clearly, as we advance we will also get clarity, always moving from what is usually said in a jumbled fashion to a more perspicuous view. There is a difference in every inquiry between arguments that are said in a philosophical way and those that are not. Hence we must not think that it is superfluous for the political person to engage in the sort of reflection that makes perspicuous not only the "that" but also the "why": for this is the contribution of the philosopher in each area.

—Aristotle, *Eudemian Ethics*

Ahmedabad, in Gujarat, is the textile-mill city where Mahatma Gandhi organized labor in accordance with his principles of non-violent resistance. Tourists visit it for its textile museum and its Gandhi ashram. But today it attracts attention, too, as the home of another resistance movement: the Self-Employed Women's Association (SEWA), with more than 50,000 members, which for over twenty years has been helping female workers in the informal sector to improve their living conditions through credit, education, and a labor union. On one side of the polluted river that bisects the city is the shabby old building where SEWA was first established, now used as offices for staff. On the other side are the education offices and the SEWA bank, newly housed in a marble office building. All the customers and all the employees are women.[1]

Vasanti sits on the floor in the meeting room of the old office building. A tiny dark woman in her early thirties, she wears an attractive electric-blue sari, and her long hair is wound neatly into a bun on the top of her head. Soft and round, she seems more comfortable sitting than walking. Her teeth are uneven and discolored, but otherwise she looks in reasonable health. My colleague Martha Chen tells me later she is a Rajput, that is, of good caste; I've never figured out how one would know that. She has come with her older (and lower-caste) friend Kokila, maker of clay pots and a janitor at the local conference hall, a tall, fiery community organizer who helps the police identify cases of domestic violence. Vasanti speaks quietly, looking down often as she speaks, but there is animation in her eyes.

Vasanti's husband was a gambler and an alcoholic. He used the household money to get drunk, and when he ran out of that money he got a vasectomy in order to take the cash incentive payment offered by local government. So Vasanti has no children to help her. Eventually, as her husband became more abusive, she could live with him no longer and returned to her own family. Her father, who used to make Singer sewing-machine parts, has died, but her brothers run an auto-parts business in what used to be his shop. Using a machine that used to be her father's, and living in the shop itself, she earned a small income making eye-holes for the hooks on sari tops. Meanwhile, her brothers gave her a loan to get the machine that rolls the edges of the sari; but she didn't like being dependent on them, because they are married and have children, and may not want to support her much longer. With the help of SEWA, therefore, she got a bank loan of her own to pay back the brothers, and by now she has paid back almost all of the SEWA loan and has two savings accounts. She now earns 500 rupees a month, a decent living, and is eager to get more involved in the SEWA union.[2] Usually, she says, women lack unity, and rich women take advantage of poor women. In SEWA, by contrast, she has found a sense of community. She clearly finds pleasure in the company of Kokila, a woman of very different social class and temperament.

By now, Vasanti is animated; she is looking us straight in the eye, and her voice is strong and clear. Women in India have a lot of pain, she says, and I, I have had quite a lot of sorrow in my life. But from the pain, our strength is born. Now that we are doing better ourselves, we want to do some good for other women, to feel that we are good human beings.

Jayamma stands outside her hut in the oven-like heat of a late March day in Trivandrum, Kerala.[3] The first thing you notice about her is the straightness of her back, and the muscular strength of her movements. Her teeth are falling out, her eyes seem clouded, and her hair is thin—but she could be a captain of the regiment, ordering her troops into battle. It doesn't surprise me that her history speaks of fierce quarrels with her children and her neighbors. Her jaw juts out as she chews tobacco. An Ezhava—a lower but not "scheduled" caste—Jayamma loses out two ways, lacking good social standing but ineligible for the affirmative-action programs established by government for the lowest castes. She still lives in a squatter's settlement on some government land on the outskirts of Trivandrum. For approximately forty-five years, until her recent retirement, Jayamma went every day to the brick kiln and spent eight hours a day carrying bricks on her head, 500 to 700 bricks per day. She never earned more than five rupees a day, and employment depends upon weather. Jayamma balanced a plank on her head, stacked twenty bricks at a time on the plank, and then walked rapidly, balancing the bricks by the strength of her neck, to the kiln, where she then had to unload the bricks without twisting her neck, handing them two by two to the man who loads the kiln. Men in the brick industry typically do this sort of heavy labor for a while and then graduate to the skilled (but less arduous) tasks of brick molding and kiln loading, which they can continue into middle and advanced ages. Those jobs pay up to twice as much, though they are less dangerous and lighter. Women are never considered for these promotions and are never permitted to learn the skills involved. Like most small businesses in India, the brick kiln is defined as a cottage industry and therefore its workers are not protected by any union. All workers are badly paid, but women suffer special disabilities. Jayamma felt she had a bad deal, but she didn't see any way of changing it.

Thus in her middle sixties, unable to perform the physically taxing job of brick carrying, Jayamma has no employment to fall back on. She is unwilling to become a domestic servant, because in her community such work is considered shameful and degrading. Jayamma adds a political explanation: "As a servant, your alliance is with a class that is your enemy." A widow, she is unable to collect a widows' pension from the government: the village office told her that she was ineligible because she has able-bodied sons, although in fact her sons refuse to support her. Despite all these reversals (and others), Jayamma is tough, defiant, and healthy. She doesn't seem interested in talking, but she shows her visitors around and makes sure that they are offered lime juice and water.

What is a philosopher doing in the slums of Trivandrum? And is there any reason to think that philosophy has anything to contribute, as such, to the amelioration of lives such as those of Vasanti and Jayamma? Our world is increasingly an interlocking world, in which we must increasingly talk with people from different cultures, classes, and backgrounds if urgent practical problems are to be solved. Among the most urgent problems are the problems of unequal nutrition and health care, unequal education, unequal vulnerability to violence, and unequal citizenship that are the current lot of many women the world over. I shall argue that philosophy does indeed have something to contribute to the guidance of public life, in ways highly relevant to shaping policies that influence these women's lives, and that one important part of philosophy's role is productive engagement with such international political debates.

Focusing on just one problem, the role of philosophy in articulating and debating norms of "the quality of life," I shall claim that philosophy provides a badly needed counterweight to simplistic approaches deriving from a certain brand of economic thought. More generally, philosophy has rich resources to offer to any policy maker who wants to think well about distributive justice in connection with women's inequality. But philosophy cannot do its job well unless it is informed by fact and experience; that is why the philosopher, although neither a field worker nor a politician, should try to get close to the reality she describes. Practice needs theory, and theory also needs practice. I begin, then, with an example of public philosophy from a project in which I have been engaged during the past thirteen years. My narrative account will illuminate, I think, both some of the potential contributions of philosophy to public life and some of the obstacles in the way of that contribution.

The project with which I have been involved was organized

through the World Institute for Development Economics Research (WIDER) of the United Nations University, a multi-disciplinary research institute located in Helsinki, Finland, which brought researchers together from many parts of the world in order to explore new approaches to the problems of developing countries. The project, organized by myself and Amartya Sen, aimed to engage philosophers and economists in conversation about the foundational concept of the quality of life. We developed and continue to develop, in different ways, an approach to quality-of-life measurement that has come to be called the "capabilities approach"; this approach argues that quality of life should be measured not in terms of satisfactions or even the distribution of resources, but in terms of what people are actually able to do and to be, in certain central areas of human functioning. We inaugurated the project at WIDER because we felt that development economics had a lot to learn from the rich philosophical debates about these questions.

When policy makers and development professionals compared countries in those days, they used to use GNP per capita as a handy measure of quality of life. This crude measure, of course, doesn't even ask about the distribution of wealth and income. Vasanti was not able to profit from Gujarat's impressive economic growth, so long as her husband denied her all control over household resources and she was untrained for any employment. Far less does this measure inquire about elements of people's lives that are important but not perfectly correlated with GNP, even when distribution has been weighed in: infant mortality, life expectancy, educational opportunities, bodily integrity, the quality of race and gender relations, the presence or absence of political and religious liberty. Even the slightly less crude economic-utilitarian move of polling people about their satisfactions does not do well enough, because people's satisfaction reports are frequently shaped by lack of information, lack of opportunity, intimidation, and sheer habit. (Vasanti used to put up with abuse: she didn't see herself as a person with the right to call the police. Jayamma didn't even think the inequalities in the brick industry were bad; they were just the way things always had been, and she didn't waste time getting upset.)

Those in the UN institute who resisted these crude GNP- and utility-based approaches did so from the point of view of a very simplistic form of postmodernist cultural relativism, one holding that no traditional cultural practice could coherently be criticized.[4] All criticism, this group held, was inevitably a form of imperialist domination. So extreme were their views that they actually criticized the introduction of the smallpox vaccination into India, on the grounds that it eradicated the cult of Sittala Devi, the goddess to whom one used to pray when one wanted to avoid smallpox!

The aim of the first phase of the quality-of-life project was to confront development economists coming out of the narrow economic-utilitarian tradition with the wealth of subtle argument on these questions that philosophy had long been producing. We planned to have debate both about the adequacy of utilitarianism as a normative framework for public choice, and also about the ideas of cultural relativism and universalism that had been discussed so unclearly in the institute's anthropological project. We also planned to focus on two specific issues—health and sex equality—that seemed to provide valuable tests of the merits of the different approaches.[5] Ultimately, our intention was to work out the arguments against these other approaches and in favor of the capabilities approach, but we also wanted to inject a rich variety of philosophical debates and positions into the arena of development economics.

Why did I think philosophy would help us make progress on these issues? The simplistic aspects of a simple relativist approach to culture have been criticized from within anthropology and sociology themselves, where scholars now increasingly stress the fact that cultures are not homogeneous but complex, not tranquil but suffused with conflict.[6] The assumptions of development economics have been criticized from within economics (for example, by feminist economists working on bargaining models of the family[7]), and also by scholars in political science and sociology. To some extent, then, the shortcomings we found in both groups of opponents might have been addressed simply by bringing in different social scientists. We did use such thinkers in our project.[8] But we gave philosophers a central role from the beginning. One immediate reason for this decision was that our anthropological opponents themselves, like other postmodernist relativists, had used appeals to philosophical authority to underwrite their claims. Without going over any arguments, they had proceeded as if the very name of Derrida, or of Foucault, could show that these issues had been settled. In gaining a hearing for our universalist proposal, therefore, we needed to show the real dimensions and complexity of the philosophical debate and to provide philosophical backing for universalism. But there were two deeper reasons for introducing philosophy into the world of development economics.

The first is that, on foundational issues such as relativism and universalism or the pros and cons of utilitarianism, philosophers generally produce more rigorous and elaborate arguments than are typically found in the social sciences. There is, of course, no orthodoxy among philosophers on such questions, but debates are typically refined and developed in such a way that real progress is made: the issues are clearly demarcated, many untenable contenders are ruled out, and so forth, until we understand the competing proposals and the arguments that support them with considerable clarity. This happens far less, I believe, in other related fields. There is no shortage of discussion of cultural relativism in the social sciences, for example; but it is usually not as systematic, rigorous, or wide-ranging as the debate in philosophy, which typically draws together considerations from the philosophy of science, the philosophy of language, and the philosophy of mind in order to illuminate the complex issues of culture. In general, philosophy in our culture has high standards of rigor and refinement in argument; debates on related issues in other professions often seem sloppy by comparison, or lacking in a set of distinctions that have already enabled philosophers to make progress.

Nor is this simply an accident of professional evolution. Philosophers in the Western tradition are the heirs of Socrates. They have a commitment to the critical scrutiny of arguments that makes them good at refining distinctions, detecting fallacies, and doing the kind of work that all thinkers about society—and, indeed, at some level all citizens—should be doing but often don't do.[9] It's not obvious that other disciplines really believe that "The unexamined life is not worth living for a human being," or that rhetoric is inferior to the humble search for correct accounts. Philosophy, while certainly not without its own pockets of dogmatism and blindness, tries hard to live in the spirit of the Socratic ideal, and does so not too badly.[10]

The second reason for making philosophy central to a project on international development can also be traced to the example of Socrates. Philosophers ask the "What is it?" question. Every academic profession has its core concepts, and all make at least some attempt to define them. But philosophy, from its start, has been that irritating gadfly that keeps asking questions about the core concepts—both its own and (irritatingly, but valuably) those of other disciplines and people. Sometimes this function has been understood in too narrow a way: as if, for example, moral philosophy should engage only in "conceptual analysis" and not in the construction and refinement of theories; or as if conceptual analysis of the most relevant sort did not require attention to empirical facts.

But if we have a sufficiently subtle and inclusive understanding of the "What is it?" question, it seems right to think that its pursuit is one of the central tasks of our discipline.

Thus many other disciplines, especially economics, concern themselves with the ideas of utilitarianism; but it falls to philosophy, above all, to ask what this theory is, how it is related to other ethical theories, and how to define each of the core concepts on which it relies. Other disciplines concern themselves with ideas of human flourishing, of "the good life," but it is the special job of philosophy to ask what exactly that obscure notion might be, and how we might adjudicate the debate among different rival specifications of it. Other disciplines (for example, law and public policy) use notions of freedom and responsibility and have some working definitions of these notions; but it falls to philosophy to think through the "What is it?" question here too, debating the merits of various different ways of conceiving of these obscure and difficult notions, until by now a highly refined set of alternatives has been worked out, of which legal and political academics are usually only dimly aware. Economists and political scientists are all the time talking about preference, choice, and desire. But it is the special job of philosophy to provide a perspicuous investigation of these foundational concepts, distinguishing desire from intention, emotion, impulse, and other psychological items, asking questions about the relation of each of these to belief and learning, and so forth. By pursuing these inquiries, philosophy has, again, evolved a highly refined account of the alternatives in this area, and its accounts show that many aspects of at least some parts of economics rest on a foundation that is not just crude, but also highly unreliable.[11] Again, thinkers in a variety of fields have shown sympathy with the capabilities approach; but it falls to philosophy to investigate more precisely the all-important distinction between capability and functioning,[12] and related distinctions between different types of human capabilities.[13]

Martha C. Nussbaum

Finally, philosophy characteristically, and far more than other fields, asks the "What is it?" question of its own methods and inquiries, asking, for example, what justification is in political theory, or what judgments, intuitions, or emotions a political argument might reasonably rely on. These questions are rarely asked with comparable pertinacity and subtlety in other disciplines concerned with social life.

These conceptual inquiries are sometimes viewed as examples of obsessive intellectual fussiness; they have, however, important practical consequences, which need to be taken into account in practical political programs. This can be shown in many areas. But to stick to the capabilities approach, the distinction between capabilities and functioning is of the greatest practical importance: a policy that aims at a single desired mode of functioning will often be quite different from one that tries to promote opportunities for citizens to choose that function or not to choose it. Thus, a policy aimed at urging all women to seek employment outside the home will be very different from a policy that aims at giving all women the choice to work outside the home or not to do so. Both policies will need to protect women from discrimination in employment and from intimidation and harassment in the employment process. But the latter, unlike the former, will also need to attend to the social meaning of domestic labor, promoting a sense that a traditional domestic life is worthwhile and consistent with human dignity; it will also need to make such choices economically feasible for women, and not unduly risky, by attending to the economic value of domestic labor when calculating settlement after divorce.

Similarly, it seems very important to distinguish several different types of human capabilities: a policy that aims simply at putting people in the internal state to function well (what I call "internal capabilities") will often be very different from a policy that aims both at creating the internal prerequisites of functioning and at shaping the surrounding material and social environment so that it is favorable for the exercise of choice in the relevant area (what I call "combined capabilities," because they represent the combination of internal capabilities with suitable external conditions). If this distinction between internal and combined capabilities is not clearly made, the merits of different policy choices will probably not be clearly debated. Thus, a policy aimed at promoting only the internal capability for freedom of expression would need only to educate people; it would not need to construct circumstances in which they can actually speak freely without penalty. A policy aimed at women's internal capability for employment outside the home would need to focus only on education and skills training; policy aimed at the combined capability would need to focus, as well, on nondiscrimination in hiring, on sexual harassment, and on protecting women from threat and intimidation from members of their own family. The "What is it?" question, in short, is profoundly practical. In its absence, public life will be governed by "what is usually said in a jumbled fashion," as Aristotle so nicely put this point.[14]

Aristotle used this Socratic idea of philosophy to argue that philosophy is an important part of the equipment of every person who aims to take an active role in public life. And for the two reasons I have given here, I believe, with him, that philosophy is an essential part of the training of any citizen who will need to deliberate with other citizens, vote, serve on a jury, or just think clearly in areas involving debates and concepts such as the ones I have mentioned. I have therefore argued elsewhere that two semesters of philosophy should be part of the undergraduate liberal arts education of every college or university undergraduate.[15] But even those who are not persuaded by that educational proposal should acknowledge, I believe, that philosophers are badly needed in academic deliberations about public policy, as critical scrutinizers of arguments and as obsessive pursuers of the foundational concepts and questions. For here, if anywhere, it is important to seek rigor and conceptual clarity. To perform their role successfully, however, philosophers will have to overcome two obstacles, one created by the resistance of economics to foundational criticism, the other by philosophy's own professional habits.

Our first conference assembled a distinguished group of philosophers, all of whom did interesting work.[16] But in two related ways the conference, which was supposed to provide policy makers and development workers with a new conceptual basis for their efforts, seemed to me a failure. Both involved the reluctance of specialists to go beyond the models and vocabularies they standardly use in writing for fellow specialists. First, we more or less entirely failed to get leading economists to take the philosophical critique of their foundations seriously. The philosophers in our group were deliberately chosen for diversity of views; they included Utilitarians, Kantians, and neo-Aristotelians. We wanted, indeed, to highlight arguments that could be made for and against the capabilities approach. But even the Utilitarian philosophers had many conceptual and foundational criticisms to make of economic welfarism; in many respects the type of Utilitarianism defended by the philosophers who wished to defend it was far closer to neo-Aristotelianism and Kantianism, as a result of debates that have unfolded over the decades, than it was to the simpler form of Utilitarianism dominant in neoclassical economics. There was unanimous agreement among the philosophers that the foundations of economics need thorough rethinking.

Those criticisms, however, had little effect. With the exception of John Roemer, who has long since been a quasi-philosopher, no economists seemed to understand that what we were saying had implications for the ways in which they should build their models. The general reaction was, "You have a very interesting profession there," or (still worse), "Sen is now doing philosophy, not economics." As Roemer observed at the conference, economists are highly committed to their models, which involve a great deal of formal sophistication; frequently they are selected for success in the profession in accordance with formal ability. If people just talk ordinary language and don't present them with alternative models, they are not likely to switch over to a new way of thinking about things, especially if it involves jettisoning formal work in which a lot has been invested. The philosophical recalcitrance of economists, and their refusal to admit that their work does make substantive philosophical commitments that need to be scrutinized, continues to be one of the greatest barriers to philosophy's effective participation in public life.

But the philosophers had problems too. The people in our team did good work; and yet they did not altogether fulfill their assignment. Sen and I commissioned the papers (with very generous stipends), asking people to spend time familiarizing themselves with pertinent pieces of the development literature so that they could relate their abstract discussions to these debates. We also asked them to address an audience of policy makers and nonspecialists. Nonetheless, people have a marked tendency to present the work that they are doing anyway, and philosophers are in the habit of addressing their peers rather than the general public. I see no reason why the issues of our project cannot be discussed, at a high degree of sophistication, in clear and jargon-free language, with concrete factual or narrative examples.[17] But philosophers need to have more practice in this type of writing if they are to do it effectively. The fact that such writing is not rewarded by the profession or encouraged in graduate programs poses an obstacle to philosophy's public influence.

In subsequent phases of the project, we focused more narrowly on women's life quality and on the issue of cultural relativism. Since the research division of that institute was cut back and changed its focus, I have continued related work under other auspices, and I have recently published a book defending a universal account of women's quality of life which makes capability and functioning the basis for quality-of-life measurement and for policy making in developing countries.[18] Increasingly, I have felt the need to get to know one region of the world well, and I have therefore done fieldwork in India, focusing in particular on women's self-employment and credit. It was during one of these visits that I came to know Vasanti and Jayamma.

Now, therefore, I return to these two women. What is the relevance of this practical work to theorizing? And what, in turn, do these lives need that theory might supply?

As Strether says in Henry James's *The Ambassadors*, "There's all the indescribable: what one gets only on the spot." How Vasanti's eyes look up and look down; the muscles of Jayamma's neck; how each poor woman does her daily accounting; how the air around her smells and tastes: these things have a bearing on a theory of gender justice. The feminist dictum that we must "start from women's experience" does not seem to me altogether correct. We won't learn much from what we see if we do not bring to our field work such theories of justice and human good as we have managed to work out until then; and one thing good theory tells us is the extent to which deprivation, ignorance, and intimidation corrupt experience itself, making it a very incomplete guide to what ought to be done. Nonetheless, it is also plain that most philosophers know little about the lives of impoverished women, especially in developing countries, and can't even imagine those lives without seeing and learning a lot more than philosophers typically do. Even the debate between cultural relativism and universalism has an empirical component. Our answers will properly be influenced by answers to empirical questions such as: how much internal debate and plurality do traditional cultures contain? What common needs and strivings do we find when we look at the lives of people in many parts of the world? And what do women say about their lives when they are in a setting characterized by freedom from fear and freedom from hierarchical authority? The fact that we look for those answers rather than the answers women give when they are in fear or cowed by authority shows that we are proceeding with a prima facie theory as we work; nonetheless, these provisional fixed points might themselves be called into question as a result of what we discover.

We would, then, need experience even if we already knew the right questions to ask. But experience is also often required to get the right questions onto the table. Theories of justice have standardly avoided the thorny question of the distribution of resources and opportunities within the family;[19] some have treated the family as a private sphere of love and care into which the state should not meddle. John Rawls is an honorable exception to both of these failings, and yet his view of the family, now presented in an article in the *The Law of Peoples*, does not offer everything that feminists would wish. In particular, by treating the family as similar to a church or a university for the purposes of political justice, Rawls appears not to carry through the implications of his own insight that the family is part of "the basic structure of society," that is, one of those institutions that affect people's life chances pervasively and from the start, and that therefore have an especially strong claim to be regulated by principles of justice.[20] So a lot of philosophical work remains to be done; and getting the questions properly raised requires experience of the constraints that unjust family structures do impose on women in many different parts of the world. To cite another example, very pertinent to Vasanti's life, sex-specific issues such as domestic violence and marital rape have not always been on the table in philosophy—although Mill is a distinguished exception to this claim. We should insist that theories of justice come to grips with the problems women face in the family and in the larger society, and should make recommendations for their solution. Philosophers need Vasanti and Jayamma, then, to goad them to ask some central questions that have not always been asked.

Feminist philosophy, of course, has tackled such women's issues. And yet it has frequently stopped well short of the international women's movement itself, by focusing much of its energy on the problems of middle-class women in America rather than on the urgent needs and interests of poor women in the developing world. A more international focus will not require feminist philosophy to turn away from its traditional themes, such as employment discrimination, domestic violence, sexual harassment, and the reform of rape law; these are all as central to women in developing countries as to Western women. But feminism will have to add new topics to its agenda if it is to approach the developing world in a productive way; among these topics are hunger and nutrition, literacy, land rights, the right to seek employment outside the home, child marriage, and child labor. These topics raise philosophical questions. To deal with them well, we need to think about how care and love of various forms play a role in women's lives; about the various forms of affective ties that form the structure of societies of various types; about the relation between property and self-respect. Thinking about these practical issues also shapes what we shall want to say about these more abstract topics. But to approach these issues well, feminist philosophers will have to learn a lot more than most Americans know about the variety of religious and cultural traditions, and about the political, legal, and economic structures of nations in which large numbers of poor women dwell.[21] In short, even feminist philosophers, whose theories have been unusually responsive to and shaped by practice, need to look at Vasanti and Jayamma, and to consider the challenge their lives pose to thought.

My own confrontation with lives such as those of Vasanti and Jayamma has changed my thinking in several important ways. The first is that I now stress far more than I had done previously the importance of property rights, access to credit, and opportunities to seek employment outside the home as capabilities valuable in themselves, and strongly linked to others, such as the ability to preserve one's bodily integrity, the ability to think and plan for oneself. Perhaps because I have been teaching in Chicago, where one hears so much about property rights every day, often in a manner that shows little compassion for the poor, I had tended to underrate the importance of property rights in poor women's lives. Everywhere I went, however, I heard women saying that having equal land rights (as women do not currently under the Hindu legal code) and having access to credit are crucial determinants of their life quality. Ela Bhatt, SEWA's founder, has powerfully linked this issue with the Gandhian conception of self-sufficiency in an anti-colonial struggle. Indeed, I have learned to value the concept of self-sufficiency more than I had previously. In defending liberal individualism against feminist objections, I had insisted, somewhat defensively, that an interest in promoting the dignity and opportunities of each person does not entail valuing self-sufficiency as a normative goal.[22] I now understand the value this norm can have when one is accustomed to a life in which one's survival depends on the good will of others.

A second important change is a greater emphasis on the Kantian ideas of dignity and non-humiliation, which had been implicit in the notion of practical reason I developed in the capabilities account but which I had insufficiently stressed. My Aristotelian starting point was helpful for the way in which it fostered attention to a variety of meaningful forms of affiliation and friendship, especially forms based on equality. The importance of friendship was amply confirmed by my experiences in women's collectives, where it is hard to convey the delight of women like Vasanti who join with other women in groups based on equality rather than families based on hierarchy and fear. However, one would be missing something of great importance if one did not add that a crucial constituent of these friendships is a shared interest in dignity and in avoiding humiliation.[23] Thinking about this is essential to thinking well about how women can be integrated into a previously all-male workplace, and about their political capabilities.

Finally, to return to friendship, my experience in India showed me the great political importance of groups of affiliation among women as sources of self-respect, friendship, and delight. Western political theory has typically been provincial when it has made "the family," as imagined in a Western nuclear form, the primary source of affection and love and of the education of children. Western feminism, although critical of much in the tradition, including its use of the distinction between public and private, has reflected this emphasis. We typically speak as if the family is the main source of intimate caring and affiliation. Communitarian thinkers within feminism are especially likely to focus on such nuclear ties and to neglect the role of other forms of affiliation and care. And yet women's groups are highly traditional as primary sources of affiliation in many parts of the world: especially in sub-Saharan Africa, their foundational role in the economy and in women's sense of selfhood is extremely clear.[24] Even when they are not so traditional, they may quickly come to play a major role in women's affective lives, showing them forms of non-hierarchical and mutually supportive attachment that they have not known in their previous lives.

Communitarians, both feminist and non-feminist, frequently speak as if we have to choose between a critical feminism that supports each person's demand for dignity and rights, and the rich emotional bonds of the family. Such thinkers are frequently worried about the way in which critical feminist projects may erode the values that hold communities together. We can easily see that traditional community values are not always so good for women. We can now add that universalist values build new types of community. A young widow in rural Bangladesh, enrolled in a literacy project that brought together women who had formerly been relatively secluded, expressed her delight vividly: "The group helped us and taught us many things. I have learned how to live unitedly. Before if any rich person abused or criticized, we could not reply. But now if anybody says anything bad, we, the 17 members of the group, go together and ask that person why he or she passed this comment. This is another kind of help we have gotten. Before we did not know how to get together and help each other. Each one was busy with their own worries and sorrows, always thinking about food for their children and themselves. Now we, the 17 members of the group, have become very close to one another."[25] This story is no isolated phenomenon. In women's groups I have visited, the first benefit typically mentioned is that of affiliation and friendship with other women in pursuit of common goals. This shows us something highly pertinent to the communitarian longing for connection that frequently animates critiques of feminism. We do not have to choose between "the embedded life" of community and a deracinated type of individualism. Universal values build their own communities, communities of resourcefulness, friendship, and agency embedded in the local scene but linked in complex ways to groups of women in other parts of the world. For these women, the new community is a lot better than the one they had inhabited before. Indeed, frequently Western feminists, with their intense interest in the couple and the nuclear family, are regarded as narrow and parochial by third-world women and are thought, in particular, to stress the sexual tie too much, in relation to other forms of affiliation.

These are difficult issues for Western feminists to ponder, for they lie very deep in many people's emotions. But I believe we should be more agnostic than liberal theory currently is concerning what fundamental affective ties the "basic structure of society" should include, and in what form. The debate in liberal theory usually takes the form of asking to what extent law is involved in the construction of the family, and how far, and in what ways, it should be involved. But the centrality of something like the heterosexual nuclear family with children (perhaps with suitable extensions to recognize same-sex couples and groups of relatives) is usually taken for granted, and it is this family institution that usually gets special support as part of society's basic structure. I believe this emphasis needs rethinking. Any workable account of quality of life should surely make room for these women's collectives as one valuable specification of general goods of affiliation, and it is not clear to me that the state ought to give priority to the Western-style nuclear family over such groupings in allocating benefits and privileges. The government of India funds projects aimed at creating women's collectives, to show women how to unite and demand their rights from employers and local government. By so allocating resources they behave wisely, even though such collectives may well take over some of the functions of more traditional units.

But why does political practice need theory? What might philosophy offer to lives such as those of Vasanti and Jayamma? I have spoken of philosophy's Socratic role in asking the "What is it?" question. But I plainly see the contribution of philosophy as requiring not only Socratic questioning but also constructive theory-building. I must say more, then, to explain how I see that further role. This is a long and difficult question, and I can only begin to sketch an answer to it.[26] The first thing we must say here, returning to my narrative of the quality-of-life project, is this: that theory is in those lives already, frequently in a bad way.

International development economics, for example, has a tremendous impact on people's lives, because its theories have a great influence on development practice and on the formation of public policy. More generally, economics has influence the world over, not only as a source of prediction but, frequently, as a source of normative guidance as well. It is very common for economists to slide over from the explanatory/predictive mode into a normative mode, although nothing in their training or argumentative practice really equips them to justify norms for public policy. Thus, when we see wealth maximization proposed as a goal of a good legal system;[27] when we see the maximization of satisfaction used as a goal in the selection of public policy on education or population; when we see GNP per capita used as an index of "the quality of life"—economists are playing the role of normative theoretical guide, a role that they typically do not play with great subtlety. Even their predictive work is sometimes marred by conceptual crudeness or questionable motivational assumptions in ways that can at times affect the models' predictive value.[28] They typically take philosophical positions on a variety of contested issues, though usually without realizing that they are doing so or providing arguments for the position taken.

As I have suggested, economists are not readily receptive to philosophical critique; but this is all the more reason why philosophers need to enter the public arena and make these points to policy makers, legal thinkers, and development workers. We need to get people thinking about the adequacy or inadequacy of utilitarian criteria of well-being; about the commensurability or incommensurability of values; about the relationship between well-being and agency; about the structure of political liberalism and the role of ideas of the good in a liberalism of this type; about the relationship between resources and human functioning; about cultural relativism and its critique; and much more. Policy makers, leaders of nongovernmental organizations, development workers: all these people, like the students we teach, are thinking and wondering about these issues already, but usually in a confused and unsystematic way. They can join in philosophical debates about these issues—if the

Martha C. Nussbaum

arguments are presented in a clear and accessible form. In this way, philosophers can try to shape development practice even without converting the economists!

It is not easy to reach this broader audience, and frequently one must work on several different levels, presenting material in one way for an audience that would like to know exactly how the approach is related to Rawls's political liberalism, another way for an audience that just wants to see the approach in its general outlines. But there is no reason why a philosopher cannot reach a broad international audience, if enough attention is devoted to writing. In the past, philosophers such as John Stuart Mill and William James were also distinguished writers for a general educated public. These are good examples for our profession to emulate. If we don't, many public debates will go on without philosophical input.

This emphatically does not mean that philosophers should stop doing systematic philosophy and become essayists or politicians. Of course they may do this, in this area and in others. Some philosophers, for example Bertrand Russell, have in effect had two careers, the philosophical work being quite far removed from the public political contribution. But there is a different contribution to political practice that philosophy can make only by remaining itself, that is, concerned with conceptual subtleties and the clear articulation of distinctions, concerned with systematic argument and theory construction. It is precisely because philosophers have thought with such subtlety and rigor about the nature of well-being and the foundations of human action that they are equipped to cogently criticize the foundations of economics. When Seneca said that the philosopher should be a "lawyer for humanity," he meant that highly abstract ideas about the nature of anger, the social origins of greed, and so on needed to be brought to bear on the real-world political scene, giving it a critical apparatus it did not have before, names of abuses that were not named before, and so forth.[29] But these ideas would enrich the political scene, giving it something it didn't have already, only if they were presented with the cogent and patient arguments characteristic of philosophy. Philosophy that moves to the practical "bottom line" too quickly fails to deliver its characteristic practical benefits. These benefits require systematizing intuitions, sorting for consistency and fit, and articulating clearly the outlines of concepts that are usually employed in a muddy fashion.

Political people often become impatient with philosophers because of their interest in patient argumentation and systematic theory-building. They want a quick move to the "bottom line," and if they can't see an immediate relation to the practical, they tend to assume that one cannot be found. Philosophers find this response painful. They do not like to be treated as ivory tower elitists who have nothing useful to offer. They are therefore sorely tempted either to withdraw, or to stop doing real philosophy, in order to accede to the demand for something immediately useful. Marx's doctoral dissertation (about the Hellenistic philosophers) contains an eloquent warning about this state of affairs:

> When philosophy turns itself as will against the world of appearance, then . . . it has become one aspect of the world which opposes another. Its relationship to the world is that of reflection. Inspired by the urge to realize itself, it enters into tension against the other. The inner self-containment and completeness has been broken. What was inner light has become consuming flame turning outwards. The result is that as the world becomes philosophical, philosophy also becomes worldly, that its realization is also its loss, that what it struggles against on the outside is its own inner deficiency.[30]

In other words, to the extent that the philosopher engages in political action, she risks losing the unworldly qualities of precision, self-containment, and reflectiveness that inform her characteristic mode of activity.

I agree with Marx to this extent: when we enter into politics, we do run some risk of losing the characteristic philosophical virtues (I believe that Cicero and Seneca sometimes, though certainly not always, show such defects). But there is no reason this *must* happen, and (perhaps unlike Marx) I believe that we should try hard to stop it from happening. We need to keep reminding ourselves that philosophers are not especially likely to be good politicians. Cicero, Seneca, Marcus Aurelius, and Karl Marx offer distinguished examples of the combination, but more often the professional training of philosophers makes them ill-suited to a world of political action. They become too interested in how things really are and not enough in how they will sound; they would rather make a distinction that can survive scrutiny than one that will bring about a politically valuable result.[31] Philosophers charged with uselessness, then, had better not jettison philosophy and take up political speech-making (unless they think they have a special talent for that, to some extent independent of their philosophical ability). More often, we should conclude that what we do best by training is also the best thing we have to offer to practice: systematic accounts that convey an overall understanding of a domain of human affairs, in such a way that intuitions are brought to bear on a practical problem in a new manner.

The Hellenistic philosophers make a valuable point in this regard. Whether in law or medicine or politics, they say, if you give a lot of prescriptions at an intermediate level of generality, you will not necessarily understand the rationale behind the prescriptions and you will be at a loss to prescribe for a new case of some complexity. You will tend to be rigid, afraid to depart from the rule. If, on the other hand, you seek a deeper and more general understanding of what generates the concrete prescriptions—if you really understand the concepts involved and can connect them in a systematic way—you will be in a far better position to face the new case, especially where the existing prescriptions are ambiguous or incomplete. That, I think, is how we should understand philosophy's potential contribution to the law, to medicine, to development policy: it provides the type of foundational and systematic understanding that can guide prescriptions and laws. Philosophy has to be grounded in experience and concerned with practice, or it will rightly be dismissed as irrelevant. Vasanti and Jayamma were not in my mind before I met them, and to that extent my mind was ill-prepared for its theoretical task. But the commitment to reality does not entail that philosophy should not also be abstract, theoretical, and concerned with conceptual distinctions. Only by retaining these concerns can it make a distinctive practical contribution.[32]

But can we reasonably have any hope that this philosophical work may bear fruit, in the world of our present and future? Kant observed that it is very difficult, looking at the evil in the world, to sustain the hopes for human progress that are probably necessary to support us in work that is aimed at practical change. But he also argues that we may adopt some optimistic beliefs as "practical postulates," precisely in order to support our continued engagement with humanity: "History may well give rise to endless doubts about my hopes, and if these doubts could be proved, they might persuade me to desist from an apparently futile task. But so long as they do not have the force of certainty, I cannot exchange my duty . . . for a rule of expediency which says that I ought not to attempt the impracticable. . . . And however uncertain I may be and may remain as to whether we can hope for anything better for mankind, this uncertainty cannot detract from the maxim I have adopted, or from the necessity of assuming for practical purposes that human progress is possible. This hope for better times to come, without which an earnest desire to do something useful for the common good would never have inspired the human heart, has always influenced the activities of right-thinking people."[33]

Feminist philosophers have special difficulty taking up Kant's practical postulate, because in all cultures throughout history the inequality of women has been an established fact of life. And despite the impressive progress women made in the twentieth century, there is still no country in which women enjoy a standard of life quality fully equal to that of men. In many nations, the gap between women and men is not closing, and is even increasing.[34] As the lives of Vasanti and Jayamma illustrate, women continue to suffer pervasive discrimination with respect to all the major human capabilities, including life itself. So a feminist philosopher might not unreasonably judge that "history" does indeed "give rise to endless doubts about [her] hopes," and that the task she attempts is indeed futile.

But it seems to me that Kant is right. The large-scale practical task is too important not to be attempted. And so long as there is no certainty that it will prove futile, it is morally valuable to entertain those hopeful thoughts about human goodness that will sustain us in our work.

Notes

I am grateful to John Deigh and Cass Sunstein for comments on an earlier draft of this chapter.

1. For a history of SEWA, see Kalima Rose, *Where Women are Leaders: The SEWA Movement in India* (Delhi: Vistaar, 1992), 172–74.

2. The amount of maintenance allotted to destitute women under India's Criminal Procedure Code was 180 rupees per month in 1986.

3. Unlike Vasanti, Jayamma has already been studied in the development economics literature. See the chapter "Jayamma, the Brick Worker," in Leela Gulati, *Profiles in Female Poverty: a Study of Five Poor Working Women in Kerala* (Delhi: Hindustan Publishing Company, 1981), and Leela Gulati and Mitu Gulati, "Female Labour in the Unorganised Sector:

The Brick Worker Revisited," *Economic and Political Weekly* May 3, 1997, 968–71, also published in Martha A. Chen (ed.), *Widows in India: Social Neglect and Public Action* (New Delhi: Sage, 1998).

4. Whether, strictly speaking, either relativism or postmodernism supports this conclusion may be doubted, since in the cases in question resistance and critique were deeply indigenous to the culture in question— as the SEWA movement, with its roots in Gujarat's Gandhian traditions, shows.

5. Although our first conference group, in 1987, consisted primarily of philosophers and economists, we also included two Scandinavian sociologists who had been using a plural metric of life quality similar to the one we were inclined to support.

6. For just two valuable recent examples of such an approach, see John L. and Jean Comaroff, *Of Revelation and Revolution: The Dialectics of Modernity on a South African Frontier* (Chicago: University of Chicago Press, vol. 1, 1991, vol. 2, 1997); and, showing division and conflict even in a community generally imagined as especially peaceful and homogeneous, Fred Kniss, *Disquiet in the Land: Cultural Conflict in American Mennonite Communities* (New Brunswick: Rutgers University Press, 1997).

7. See Amartya Sen, "Gender and Cooperative Conflicts," in *Persistent Inequalities,* ed. I. Tinker (New York: Oxford, 1991), 123–49, and Partha Dasgupta, *An Inquiry into Well-Being and Destitution* (Oxford: Clarendon Press, 1993), chapter 11. For other useful examples of bargaining approaches, see Bina Agarwal, *A Field of One's Own: Gender and Land Rights in South Asia* (Cambridge: Cambridge University Press, 1994), and "Bargaining and Gender Relations: Within and Beyond the Household," FCND Discussion Paper, International Food Policy Research Institute, March 1997; Shelly Lundberg and Robert A. Pollak, "Bargaining and Distribution in Marriage," *Journal of Economic Perspectives* 10, 139–58; and L. Chen, E. Huq, and S. D'Souza, "Sex Bias in the Family Allocation of Food and Health Care in Rural Bangladesh," *Population and Development Review* 7, 55–70.

8. Sociologists Robert Eriksson, Erik Allardt, Nancy Chodorow, and

Valentine Moghadam, anthropologist Martha Chen, political theorists Susan Moller Okin and Seyla Benhabib, economists John Roemer, Jean Dréze, Amartya Sen, and (in a related project) Partha Dasgupta, all played a role in our first two conferences; the third included, in addition, health policy and medical experts. Other WIDER projects involved still more social scientists from other disciplines.

9. For this reason, I argue in *Cultivating Humanity* that, although in principle the abilities of "Socratic self-examination" that citizens need could be imparted through courses in many different disciplines, in practice this is best done by courses in philosophy. See Martha Nussbaum, *Cultivating Humanity: A Classical Defense of Reform in Liberal Education* (Cambridge: Harvard University Press, 1997).

10. For my own understanding of the Socratic elenchus and its contribution, see my review essay of Gregory Vlastos's Socratic Studies, *The Journal of Philosophy* 94, 27–45.

11. See my "Flawed Foundations: The Philosophical Critique of (a Particular Type of) Economics," *The University of Chicago Law Review* 64, 1197–214.

12. Both Sen and I argue that respect for choice should lead us to make capability, rather than functioning, the political goal; by contrast, perfectionist liberalisms such as those of John Stuart Mill and Joseph Raz (*The Morality of Freedom,* Oxford, Clarendon, 1986) prefer to construe the goal in terms of functioning.

13. I argue that three distinct types of capabilities need to figure in the approach: basic capabilities, or the innate equipment of human beings that enables them, with sufficient support and care, to attain higher-level capabilities; internal capabilities, or states of the person that would, in suitable circumstances, prove sufficient for the exercise of the relevant functioning; and combined capabilities, or the internal state combined with suitable external circumstances for the exercise of the function. For example, a woman who has had some education and training, but who is threatened with physical violence should she leave the house to look for work, has the internal but not the combined capability to seek employment outside the house. Politics should aim at the production of combined

capabilities. For the most recent statement of this position, see Martha Nussbaum, "The Good as Discipline," in *Ethics of Consumption: The Good Life, Justice, and Global Stewardship,* ed. David A Crocker and Toby Linden (Lanham: Rowman & Littlefield, 1997).

14. Aristotle, *Eudemian Ethics* 1216a30–39: see the second epigraph that opens this chapter. Aristotle connects understanding the "why" closely to the task of giving definitions and accounts.

15. See Nussbaum, *Cultivating Humanity,* chapter 1.

16. Nussbaum and Sen (eds.), *The Quality of Life* (Oxford: Clarendon, 1993).

17. Dan W. Brock, "Quality of Life Measures in Health Care and Medical Ethics" is a fine example of such clear writing (and of research specifically responsive to our commission). Charles Taylor, "Explanation and Practical Reason," though not originally commissioned for our volume (because Taylor replaced another participant at a late date), is another extremely lucid and readable paper. It is interesting that both these authors have spent time in practical politics, and therefore know from experience what sort of writing is effective.

18. See Martha Nussbaum, *Women and Human Development: The Capabilities Approach* (Cambridge: Cambridge University Press, 2000).

19. See Susan Okin, *Justice, Gender, and the Family* (New York: Basic Books, 1989).

20. John Rawls, "The Idea of Public Reason Revisited," *University of Chicago Law Review* 64 (1997), 765–808, reprinted in Rawls, *The Law of Peoples* (Cambridge, MA: Harvard University Press, 1999), 129–80.

21. For example, in my experience almost all philosophers and legal thinkers are astounded to discover that India does not have a uniform code of civil law, and that the various religious systems of personal law manage things in the domain of property and inheritance as well as marriage, divorce, custody, and maintenance. If they don't know this, they can hardly begin to conceive of the problems women in India face, or to frame the interesting philosophical issues of sex equality and religion-free exercise in a relevant manner.

22. See *The Feminist Critique of Liberalism,* a Lindley Lecture (Law-

rence: University of Kansas Press, 1997), reprinted in Nussbaum, *Sex and Social Justice* (New York: Oxford University Press, 1999).

23. See, for example, the valuable treatment of these notions in Avishai Margalit, *The Decent Society,* trans. Naomi Goldblum (Cambridge: Harvard University Press, 1996).

24. See Nkiru Nzegwu, "Recovering Igbo Tradition: A Case for Indigenous Moments Organizations in Development," in *Women, Culture, and Development,* ed. Martha Nussbaum and Jonathan Glover (Oxford: Clarendon, 1995).

25. Martha A. Chen, *A Quiet Revolution: Women in Transition in Rural Bangladesh* (Cambridge. Schenkman, 1983), 216.

26. For further thoughts, see my "Why Practice Needs Ethical Theory: Particularism, Principle, and Bad Behavior," in *"The Path of Law" and Its Influence: The Legacy of Oliver Wendell Holmes, Jr.,* ed. Steven J. Burton (New York: Cambridge University Press, 2000).

27. See, for a typical example, Richard Posner, *The Economics of Justice* (Cambridge, MA: Harvard University Press, 1981).

28. For a more extensive treatment, see my "Flawed Foundations."

29. See my "Lawyer for Humanity: Theory and Practice in Ancient Political Thought," *Nomos* 37, 181–215.

30. Karl Marx, *Doctoral Dissertation: Difference Between the Democritean and Epicurean Philosophy of Nature,* in Karl Marx/Friedrich Engels, *Collected Works,* Vol. 1 (London: Lawrence and Wishard, 1975), 85.

31. See Dan W. Brock, *Life and Death: Philosophical Essays in Biomedical Ethics* (Cambridge: Cambridge University Press, 1993).

32. See on this point John Rawls, introduction to the paperback edition of *Political Liberalism* (New York: Columbia University Press, 1996), lxii; see also my "Why Practice Needs Ethical Theory."

33. Immanuel Kant, "On the Common Saying: 'This May Be True in Theory, but It Does not Apply in Practice,' " in *Kant: Political Writings,* ed. Hans Reiss, trans. H. B. Nisbet (Cambridge: Cambridge University Press, second edition 1991), 89. I have altered the final word of the translation, substituting "people" for his "men." The German has a substantivized adjective, "the right-thinking ones."

34. In India, for example, the ratio of women to men is the lowest it has been at any time since the census started being kept, a good index of systematic undernourishment and unequal medical care: see Jean Drèze and Amartya Sen, *India: Economic Development and Social Opportunity* (Delhi: Oxford University Press, 1995).

6

What Is Philosophy?
The Philosophical Point of View
After the End of Dogmatic Metaphysics

Karl-Otto Apel

What is Philosophy? What a question! I must confess that I was shocked and almost paralyzed at the thought of tackling this question in a book such as this. I would have no problem answering the question "What is philosophy?" for an audience of lay people.[1] I would start out with some characteristic definitions of the Greek classics that paraphrase and interpret the word *philosophia*. I would perhaps link this up with Kant's famous four questions: "What can I know?," "What should I do?," "What may I hope?," and "What is the human being?"[2] I would also make use of Kant's distinction between the "scholastic concept" (*Schulbegriff*) and the public or worldly concept (*Weltbegriff*) of philosophy. I would adopt and display these classical explications myself, especially those that do not anticipate a (metaphysical) knowledge about the "soul" or the "divine and human things" but speak only of striving for orientation toward the "ultimate purposes of reason," as Kant says.[3] But how should I answer the question "What is philosophy?" for my colleagues, who know very well what philosophy is—that is, what it has been considered to be—but nevertheless want to hear something specific about what I think it should be today?

Among the general public, there is something like a boom of interest in philosophy: registration rates for traditional philosophy courses are high, and non-traditional courses are proliferating (there are philosophy courses for business managers and even introductions to philosophy for young girls). This vast audience is well prepared to conceive of philosophy in the classical vein as a promise of orientation toward the "last purposes of reason" or as a possible answer to the four Kantian questions.

The picture of professional philosophy is quite different. Here, too, the publicly testified occupation with philosophy (the philosophy *Betrieb* in Heidegger's sense) is gigantic. In recent years, we have seen an increase of philosophical journals and books that surpasses every former period of history. But the meta-philosophical reflection of the prominent professional philosophers in Europe and North America is characterized either by skepticism or by a resolute rejection of the classical expectations evoked by the term *philo-sophy*, not only those expectations connected with *metaphysics generalis* and *specialis* in the pre-Kantian sense but also those regarding universal validity claims of (critical) reason.

A collection of essays called *After Philosophy: End or Transformation?*, edited by Baynes, Bohman, and McCarthy, clearly illustrates the current situation in professional philosophy. According to *After Philosophy* there are two broad conceptions of what philosophy still could be. The first conception calls for the "end of philosophy": Richard Rorty, Jean-François Lyotard, Michel Foucault, and Jacques Derrida all represent this avant-garde of subversion. The other conception seeks a "transformation of philosophy," of which there are two versions. Donald Davidson, Michael Dummett, Hilary Putnam, Jürgen Habermas, and I all represent the "systematic" version of transformation, while Hans-Georg Gadamer, Alasdair MacIntyre, Hans Blumenberg, and Charles Taylor all prefer a "hermeneutic, rhetoric, narrative" version of transformation.

I agree with the way *After Philosophy* divides up current metaphilosophical reflection, and I think I belong to the systematic transformation group, as that volume suggests. Nevertheless, I think it noteworthy that Baynes, Bohman, and McCarthy have some difficulties with the transcendental aspect of my "transcendental pragmatics." They say that "whatever disagreements may separate the philosophers represented here, all of them are fallibilists and finitists. None claims self-certifying necessity for philosophical insight."[4] But then the editors add in a footnote: "Apel does make one important exception to the principle of fallibilism: some pragmatic presuppositions, he argues in a transcendental vein, are unavoidable presuppositions of critical and argumentative discourse. Thus philosophical doubt only makes sense within a pragmatic framework that is itself beyond doubt."[5] This is indeed a very appropriate characterization of my views. My position is a form of "consistent fallibilism," because any unrestricted principle of fallibilism—especially self-applicable fallibilism, as it is defended by the late Popperians[6]—must abolish its own meaning.

I think philosophy should be as self-critical as possible; it should even follow a heuristics of self-suspicion in examining its own validity claims (particularly when it tries to compare its own capacities and tasks with those of the natural sciences and literature). But it should not confuse self-critical arguments with fashionable generalizations of mere feelings of resignation; all too often, such feelings erupt in pseudo-metaphysical statements concerning the finiteness and complete fallibility of our capacities of reason—statements that seem to escape all critical enquiries into their *own* validity conditions by appealing to what we allegedly can derive simply from the evidence of historical experience.

After the End of Dogmatic Metaphysics

The best antidote against such confusion, I suggest, is a constant reflective comparison of one's philosophical propositions—including the skeptical ones—with the validity claims that are implied in the speech acts by which those propositions must be brought forward. For if our philosophical propositions are not compatible with those pragmatically presupposed validity claims, we entangle ourselves in a performative self-contradiction—the post-linguistic-turn equivalent to what Kant considered a violation of the "self-consistency of reason" (*Selbsteinstimmigkeit der Vernunft*).

This suggested method of strict transcendental reflection is in our day the most radical way to use transcendental arguments in philosophy.[7] It is no longer tied up with the project of a transcendental deduction of "categorial schemes" or their semantic equivalents (as it was renewed once more by Peter Strawson and his followers).[8] Hence it is not subject to the verdict of "detranscendentalization" which Rorty derived from Davidson's questioning of the "third dogma of empiricism"—the assumption of a strict separation between the "form" and the "content" of cognition.[9] For we can and must test all kinds of philosophical arguments—even those for holism or skepticism—to make sure that we can advance them while avoiding performative self-contradiction. The fact that argumentation presupposes validity claims is the non-circumventable, and thus far transcendental, precondition of philosophy. Or may even this be called into question in our day? With this question and the preceding remarks, I have set the stage for my attempt, in what follows, to explain what I think philosophy should be today.

The "End of Philosophy" Position

Looking back to the volume *After Philosophy*, I think that those who represent the "end of philosophy" more or less explicitly dispute my thesis that argumentation presupposing certain validity claims is the non-circumventable precondition of philosophy. But because they dispute it by arguments, they are themselves still practicing philosophy in accordance with my transcendental-pragmatic minimal qualification, and their different pertinent disputings are just so many ways of committing a performative self-contradiction. This has to be analyzed in more detail with regard to its consequences.

Disputing the transcendental function of argumentation is internally connected with disputing that there are essential differences between the language games of philosophy, rhetoric, and poetry. To avoid misunderstandings, let me explain. I do not deny that great poetry can be philosophically relevant—even more so than mediocre pieces of scholastic philosophy. Neither do I oppose using rhetorical and poetical devices—for example, metaphors—in the course of philosophical argumentation. But, in my opinion, there is a limit to this legitimate fusion of language games or genres; literary or rhetorical strategies should not obscure or deny the universal validity claims of philosophical arguments—especially when those arguments should be exposed to possible criticism.

Consider, for example, the notorious ambiguity of the words *persuade, persuasion,* and *persuasive,* which in English, as in the Romance languages, derive from the Latin and thus represent the rhetorical tradition. In our day speech act theory makes it possible to draw a very clear distinction between convincing by arguments (in German: *überzeugen*), which makes the perlocutionary effect dependent on the autonomous judgment of the hearer, and "persuasion" in the narrow rhetorical sense (in German: *überreden*), which wants to reach the "perlocutionary effect" at all costs, even by cunningly preventing or eliminating the autonomous judgment of the hearer.

Even worse than the confusion between überzeugen and überreden is the confusion between two different openly strategic uses of language: using arguments strategically in the service of redeeming and criticizing validity claims, versus using language strategically in the service of one's self-interest—say, by bringing forward offers and/or threats (as, for example, in bargaining). For we can know by transcendental-pragmatic reflection that the first language game is indispensable for proving the power of arguments, whereas the latter is excluded a priori by the philosophical interest in reaching a consensus about validity claims.

In *After Philosophy*, those who represent the "end of philosophy," namely Rorty, Lyotard, Foucault, and Derrida, all ignore or dispute somehow the transcendental function of argumentation. They step beyond the limit of self-consistent philosophy, practicing and propagating not only a harmless enrichment of philosophy by elements of the literary genres, but also some of those confusions I just noted concerning rationales for the use of language.

Rorty, for example, proposes to reduce philosophy to "edifying conversation." By so doing, he tries to avoid all the intricate philosophical problems connected with the universal validity claims of argumentation. Once at a conference in Chicago, an adherent of Rorty's solution to the troubles of transcendental philosophy, after having listened to my paper on discourse rationality, told me: "You shouldn't have validity claims, you should just be persuasive." This statement accords with Rorty's peculiar consensus theory of truth, which is pragmatic in that it has its normative measure in the factual persuasive success of a claim for a particular audience. By aiming at concrete social agreements, Rorty wants to replace our striving for "objectivity" with a striving for "solidarity," and (following William James) to understand by "truth" whatever is "good to believe" for those who can in fact come to agreement—for example, "the liberal, educated members of the western society" standing in the tradition of occidental culture.[10] Rorty's view seems to be a culture-centric equation of the true with the useful by rhetorical argumentation; it

Karl-Otto Apel

undercuts or dissolves the idea of the truth-claim as a claim to a universal validity independent of contextual persuasive success.

Indeed, Rorty expressly denies that the distinction between überreden and überzeugen has anything to do with the difference between "context-dependence" and "universality" (of a truth-claim). For him, "the distinction between the strategic and the non-strategic use of language is just the distinction between cases in which all we care about is convincing others and cases in which we hope to learn something." These cases for Rorty are "two ends of a spectrum, at one end of which we shall use any dirty trick we can (lying, *omissio veri, suggestio falsi,* etc.) to convince. [I would have expected the word *persuade* here, because I (following Socrates) connect any attempt at convincing by argument with the hope of learning something.] At the other end we talk to others as we talk to ourselves when we are most at ease, most reflective, and most curious . . . 'the pure pursuit of truth' is a traditional name for the sort of conversation which takes place at one end of this spectrum. But I do not see what that sort of conversation has to do with universality or with unconditionality."[11]

However, in a serious philosophical discussion, such a "pragmatic" position makes it impossible to be criticized by an opponent, because it is not prepared to expose a validity claim that could be distinguished in advance from the context-dependent success of persuasion. By eliminating the possibility of criticism, Rorty's conversationalist pragmatism marks, indeed, the end of philosophy. Karl Popper was right to consider immunization against criticism— and that is the same as having no context-independent validity claims—the deadly sin in philosophy.

But isn't Rorty's position the only way out, because there is no criterion of truth in the sense of "external realism"[12] available—that is, no criterion that could be distinguished in advance from possible success within the discourse? The alternative to Rorty's way out is not represented by any metaphysics of external realism, but rather by Charles Peirce's "pragmaticism."[13] Pragmaticism, as I understand it, is a normative proceduralism of argumentative discourse, a way of relying not on rhetorical persuasion but on a regulative idea of arguing: the idea that the ultimate consensus to be reached under ideal (epistemological and communicative) conditions of argumentative discourse *would be* identical with what we *must* understand by the truth if we suppose that truth is something we, in principle, can strive for.[14] Even though no particular community will ever actually reach a consensus that captures the whole truth about reality, any serious argument necessarily presupposes the possibility of such consensus as a *regulative idea*. In other words, we cannot argue against the presupposition of this regulative idea without implicitly committing a performative self-contradiction.

The protagonist of philosophical postmodernism, Jean-Francois Lyotard, provides a good example of how arguing against this regulative idea leads to performative self-contradiction. Following a Nietzschean or anarchistic version of Wittgensteinianism, Lyotard openly attacks the need for, or the possibility of, a "legitimation" of discourses by a philosophical meta-discourse. But he does not reflect on the unavoidability of his own philosophical meta-discourse (and its universal validity claims). Instead he suggests that the philosophical meta-discourse of modern science is like the metaphysical meta-narratives of speculative philosophy of history which originated in the eighteenth century and culminated in the work of Hegel and Marx. In both cases, a totalized claim to universal validity is made on behalf of a specific conception of the modern idea of progress. Against such views, Lyotard plays off both the insights of post-empiricist philosophy of science and the experiences of our present disillusioned age. Because he denies that there can be transcendental critique of reason, he can say things like the following: "Is legitimacy to be found in consensus obtained through discussion, as Jürgen Habermas thinks? Such consensus does violence to the heterogeneity of language games. And invention is always born of dissension. Postmodern knowledge is not simply a tool of the authorities; it refines our sensitivity to differences and reinforces our ability to tolerate the incommensurable. Its principle is not the experts' homology, but the inventor's paralogy."[15]

This characteristic passage from *The Postmodern Condition* raises questions like the following. Doesn't this very argument against the search for consensus implicitly appeal to consensus, so long, at least, as it is an argument, part of a philosophical metadiscourse which displays its character by its universal validity claim? Furthermore, how can the "heterogeneity of language games" be violated by a "consensus through discussion," since it will make the hoped-for consensus impossible? We can, and should, reach a consensus through discussion about the fact that the "heterogeneity of language games" necessarily prevents us from reaching a consensus. But in this case we would not simply celebrate "paralogy." Instead, at least in the case of science, we would try to overcome the heterogeneity of language games. We would search for a more comprehensive "paradigm" or a "complementarity principle" (as in the case of Niels Bohr). At the very least we would try to reach a consensus about the character of, and reasons for, a persistent heterogeneity of language games.

Sometimes we can reach a consensus about the fact that different cognitive interests motivate methodological differences (for example, the differences between the hermeneutically oriented humanities and the nomological-explanatory natural sciences or the quasi-nomological behavioral sciences).[16] There are also different types of rationality, as Kant showed us by distinguishing among theoretical reason, practical reason, and aesthetic judgment. However, recognizing such differences does not force us to suppose that there are no internal relations between the different dimensions of reasoning, so that, for example, as Lyotard asserts, "the goal of emancipation has nothing to do with science."[17] We can realize, for example, that in the present situation of humankind, an ethic of global justice and co-responsibility depends in crucial ways on (the progress of) scientific knowledge about ecological and socio-economic facts. I find it absurd to suppose that the consensus-postulate of a universal pragmatics of argumentative discourse would suppress the differences between the many classes of speech acts.

If, after all, we have to deal with the incommensurable differences between culture-dependent world views, including different strong ethical values, we can follow a complementarity principle of the following kind: on the one hand, in our multicultural (and ultimately global) society, we can and should agree to tolerate cultural differences; on the other hand, we can and should also agree to some universal norms—among them human rights—that restrict *pernicious* cultural idiosyncrasies (those which make it impossible for different cultures to coexist in peace or to cooperate in the face of common problems of humanity like the environmental crisis).[18]

In such cases, searching for "consensus through discussion" is vitally needed. It functions neither as a "tool of authority" nor as a tool of "terror" (as Lyotard suggests);[19] rather, it is the only possible alternative to a pure struggle of power positions in the sense of social Darwinism. Argumentative discourse opens up a free space not only for consensus but also for rational dissension—and thereby for the kinds of "innovations" and "inventions" everybody can deem desirable.

Lyotard's denunciation of the philosophical meta-discourse of legitimation provides a good example of how counter-philosophical strategies of argumentation necessarily abolish themselves through performative self-contradiction. Such contradiction is demonstrated not only by Lyotard's provocative booklet *La condition postmoderne*

Karl-Otto Apel

(1979) but also by his main work: *Le différend* (1983). There, the performative self-contradiction inherent in the "end of philosophy" view displays itself in a way that is equally transparent and irritating: it produces a constant struggle between two polar-opposite attitudes.

On the one hand, Lyotard performatively shows an emotional and evaluative favor toward particular life forms and their peculiar ways of linguistic self-expression (and world interpretation); he opposes all bureaucratic and technocratic tendencies which force peoples into conformity through language politics. In this, Lyotard, whether he believes it or not, stands in full agreement with the explicit legitimation policy of universal pragmatic discourse ethics. For this philosophical meta-discourse does not, as he supposes, prescribe any pre-fixed rules of language use but only the fundamental norm that, with regard to the use of language, all possible discourse partners have equal rights and equal responsibility.

On the other hand, in his own explicit meta-discourse, Lyotard denies any such norm. For him, all possible disputes between different validity claims of argumentation are merely different positions of a "différend," and this means: "un cas de conflit entre deux parties (au moins) qui ne pourrait pas etre tranche equitablement faute d'une regle de jugement applicable aux deux argumentations," (a case of conflict between two parties (at least) that could not be decided impartially because there is no rule of judgment applicable to both argumentations).[20] In *La condition postmoderne*, Lyotard states: "to speak is to fight in the sense of playing, and speech acts fall within the domain of general agonistics."[21] In *Le différend*, following this line, Lyotard denies that any ethical relation is inter-subjectively valid. To seriously claim a moral obligation with regard to somebody else is a "scandal," it is the *"différend par excellence."* In opposition to Kant, Lyotard asserts: the absoluteness of the moral law "alienates the I" and cunningly makes it believe that it wills its own abdication in favor of a rule of reciprocity. According to Lyotard, the acknowledgment of a "rule of consensus or of exchangeability between partners, the rule of the dialogue," is not a genuine law of freedom; it has been illegitimately transferred from theoretical to practical discourse although freedom and knowledge are separated by an "abyss." Thus Lyotard concludes that "There is no ethical community."[22]

Given Lyotard's philosophical meta-discourse, it is impossible to legitimate or criticize anything. Lyotard himself, however, passionately legitimates and criticizes many things. This primordial performative self-contradiction is the source of the subversive irritation of all the specific theses of Lyotard's postmodernism. I cannot go into detail here, but I want to emphasize that Lyotard's philosophy, in my opinion, provides the best illustration of what philosophy can be "after the end of philosophy."

The other two representatives of the "end of philosophy" view are Foucault and Derrida. Both thinkers are extremely interesting as regards the particular content of their work, but, in the context of my topic, I can only state that they further represent the present self-destruction of philosophy by performative self-contradiction.

Derrida would perhaps even confirm this assessment by claiming that there is no way open for us today other than trying to overcome occidental "logocentrism" while still exploiting its argumentative apparatus (in a sense, the later Heidegger anticipated this line of thought with his talk about overcoming occidental metaphysics through a *Verwinden der Metaphysik*). But that is no way to escape the aporia of the performative self-contradiction. In Derrida's case, for example, it simply is not feasible to dispute the possibility of presenting by signs a "transcendental signified" and thereby of communicating just this alleged fact. There must be another way to deal with Derrida's discovery of the "différance" (that is, the continuous generation of a difference of meaning) and the "dissemination" of the sign process. We can find such a way, I believe, with the aid of a Peircean semiotics which knows not only about the infinite reference of signs to other signs but also about the triadic structure of the sign function, and thus avoids Derrida's transition from semiotics to semioticism.[23]

As for Foucault, I find it even easier to esteem the discoveries of his historical inquiries without complying with his philosophical self-understanding. One may admit that in all epochal breaches of the constitution and linguistic interpretation of the social reality, an intertwinement of "jurisdiction" and "veridiction" by "truth regimes" is at work; nevertheless one may still insist on the analytical separation between the scientific will to truth and the political or quasi-political will to power. The human sciences must indeed be the subject and the object of a continual critique of ideology, but they cannot be replaced by a Nietzschean "genealogy" (of morality and truth) that abolishes its own validity claim.[24]

Indeed, in my opinion, Nietzsche is the classical initiator of that method or style of thought which, by unmasking every claim to truth and moral rightness, abolishes its own validity claim. This style of committing the performative self-contradiction does not overcome occidental metaphysics; it is rather a typical product of the anti-Platonist counter-metaphysics of naturalist reductionism, which is a metaphysical misuse of modern scientific reductive explanation.

In Schopenhauer's thought, this counter-metaphysics took the form of a functional reduction of reason. Whereas the metaphysics of German Idealism had integrated free will into reason, for Schopenhauer reason was nothing but a necessary function of the natural will—the drive or urge of life. Schopenhauer contradicted himself when he tried to explain why and how Man should negate the natural will in the interest of truth and the moral sentiment of pity (compassion). Nietzsche tried to overcome Schopenhauer's inconsistency by affirming the natural will as "will to power." But, this simply made the performative self-contradiction implicit in functional reductionism even more obvious. Ironically, the so-called philosophy of Postmodernism continues that Nietzschean reductionist counter-metaphysics—a self-abolishing inversion of Plato's hypostatization of reason or *logos* or *nous*.

Perhaps "logocentrism" (in Derrida's sense) is the kind of modern rationalism, namely objectification of the world, that Heidegger subsumes under the label *Gestell* (of science and technique) or the type of "rationalization" of modern thought that, according to Max Weber and Horkheimer/Adorno, culminates in the absolutization of "means-ends" or "instrumental" rationality. In this case, modern rationalism should be subjected to a critique from the point of view of reason. This would be no self-destructive critique of reason by reason but a critique of the modern absolutization of certain abstractive types of rationality from the point of view of the philosophical rationality of argumentative discourse.[25]

In any case, the total critique of reason mounted by the "end of philosophy" view cannot answer our questions as to what philosophy can be in our time. Hence, let us now consider the project of transforming philosophy.

Transforming Philosophy

As the preceding section shows, philosophy's non-circumventable (and thus far transcendental) presupposition is that argumentation includes universal validity claims. I note provisionally that four such claims—the meaning claim, the truth claim, the veracity claim, and the moral rightness claim—are implicit in any act of argumentation within a discourse community.[26] We cannot question these transcendental presuppositions without abolishing the performance of philosophy. Therefore, we must test all philosophical theses (especially those theses that characterize a philosophical position) to see if their propositional content is consistent with their performatively expressed validity claims. If a thesis is not consistent in this way, it abolishes itself by abolishing its meaning claim (which is presupposed by the other validity claims). This test of performative consistency provides the most radical criterion of sense-critique (*Sinnkritik*). Sense-critique, in my opinion, is the primordial method of a transcendental critique of reason after the linguistic turn of philosophy, and a method which can be represented by a reflective transcendental pragmatics of language.

We must examine the performative consistency of arguments in order to discern which theses are presupposed by the very act of arguing. We must not embrace a dogmatic transcendentalism which simply *supposes* certain claims to be performative presuppositions of argumentation (and hence immune from questioning). Because I have just provisionally enumerated the four validity claims of argumentation, one might suspect that I am guilty of such a dogmatic stance. But instead, I suggest that we use the method of sense-critique to *find out* which presuppositions of argumentation cannot be questioned without getting entangled in a performative self-contradiction (and, at the same time, cannot be grounded in the traditional sense without committing a *petitio principii*).[27]

The method of sense-critique reveals presuppositions of argumentation besides the four validity claims: for example, the presupposition of freedom of will and action,[28] the presupposition of the existence of the arguer and of an external world outside the consciousness, the presupposition of the arguer's embodiment and, in this context, of linguistic and natural signs, and so forth. These transcendental-pragmatic presuppositions of argumentation can be considered paradigmatic evidences of the specifically philosophical language game. They are distinct from the paradigmatic evidences of all other language games because virtually all the other language games can be questioned, together with their paradigmatic evidences, as being historically contingent. By contrast, the paradigmatic evidences of the philosophical language game cannot be questioned because they are the conditions of the possibility of all questioning. I shall come back to this thesis, which, I know, looks implausible to most contemporary philosophers.

The foregoing suggestions may have already made clear what I consider the vantage point of a topical type of First Philosophy: it should be a transformation of philosophy along the lines of transcendental philosophy, something in the vein of a Kantian "critique of reason" rather than of a total—and hence self-destructive—critique of reason or logocentrism. But it should also involve a radical critique of both dogmatic metaphysics and dogmatic transcendentalism. What does this mean?

In the past two centuries, it has become clear that Kant's *Critique of Pure Reason* is deeply ambiguous with regard to its message of a "revolution of the mode of philosophical thinking." On the one hand, Kant's rejection of dogmatic metaphysics and his corresponding demand for a transcendental inquiry into the conditions of the possibility of intersubjectively valid knowledge is a crucial turning point toward a novel paradigm of philosophy which still guides us today. But on the other hand, Kant could not carry through his "critical business" without entangling himself in the type of dogmatic metaphysics he wanted to call into question; therefore his system of thought has become a paradigm of dogmatic transcendentalism. In order to outline the perspective of a transcendental philosophy after the end of dogmatic metaphysics, I will make some comments about both sides of the Kantian heritage.

In my opinion, the decisive objection to the equation of philosophy with metaphysics is not that metaphysics is First Philosophy striving for an ultimate foundation of validity claims (this assessment, fashionable in our day, would question transcendental philos-

Karl-Otto Apel

ophy as well, and hence would question the possible function of an autonomous philosophy altogether). Instead, I think that philosophy cannot be metaphysics because metaphysics is dogmatic.

Ontological—or onto-theological—metaphysics since Plato and Aristotle has considered the world (that is, all being, including also the human intellect or reason) as a "limited whole" ("*ein begrenztes Ganzes*," as Wittgenstein said in the *Tractatus*[29]), as something that can be considered contingent, and hence can be looked upon and questioned from outside—from a divine standpoint—without critical reflection on the transcendental conditions of knowing. This "dogmatic" attitude of philosophizing reveals itself in two characteristic ways.

The first is a strong ontological correspondence or adequation theory of truth, belonging to the metaphysical position of "external realism." It presupposes that we could observe the subject-object relation of cognition from outside, so to speak (as if it were a relation between two inner-worldly (intra-mundane) things), and thus could check for correspondence between the intellect and the things it represents. Kant and later Franz Brentano and Frege have spelled out the aporias of such an ontological reduction of the meaning of truth.

The second characteristic testimony of the dogmatic attitude is expressed by Leibniz's famous question: "Why is there something at all and not rather nothing?" Analyzed from a Kantian point of view, this question is "illegitimate" (*überwenglich*). A legitimate *why*-question can be posed with regard to the existence of any thing within the world of our experience, but this kind of question cannot be posed legitimately with regard to the whole of the world from a standpoint outside the world. For Leibniz, taking such a standpoint was of course very well possible, and it predetermined the answer to his question—the answer of a metaphysics of Christian Platonism, according to which God has created the world *ex nihilo*.

After the End of Dogmatic Metaphysics

But if one takes seriously both Kant's rejection of such dogmatic metaphysics and his demand for critical reflection on the transcendental conditions of the possibility of valid knowledge, one quickly realizes that in working out his own "critique of reason," Kant fell far short of satisfying his own implicit standards. Kant failed to preserve the "consistency of reason" (*die Einstimmigkeit der Vernunft*) through a strictly "transcendental reflection," that is, through a continuous comparative account of the conditions of the possibility of experience and of the conditions of his own philosophical inquiry. Instead he constructed a novel type of dogmatic metaphysics which he needed in order to account for the relationships among the main parts of his philosophical system: "transcendental idealism" with regard to the form of experience, "empirical realism" with regard to the particular phenomena or appearances, and a "transcendent" background supposition of unknowable "things in themselves." The presuppositions of Kant's dogmatic metaphysics inevitably lead one to suppose (in order to understand how the validity of objective experience could come about) an illegitimate superstructure of a causal commercium between the transcendental subject or consciousness and the noumenal realm of things in themselves.

As is well known, Kant's contemporaries rightly criticized this incoherence in the Kantian system; and Hegel, I suggest, focused his critique on the crucial condition of a radical and self-consistent transcendental philosophy, namely, on that conception of valid knowledge that is presupposed by the critical philosopher himself.[30] I think Hegel was completely right in claiming that the critical philosopher cannot examine the functions of cognition without entering into that business himself; in short: philosophers must deem themselves capable of knowing the real substance both of things and of the intellect (rather than mere appearances of the outer and/or inner senses).

Karl-Otto Apel

{ 170 }

But Hegel went far beyond a critical reconstruction of the conception of transcendental philosophy. He not only rejected the Kantian distinction between phenomena and noumena but also abolished Kant's distinction between scientific knowledge in the modern empirical sense and knowledge of a transcendental epistemology. Instead he restored the Platonic conception of philosophical science as *episteme;* and he tried to realize this conception by conceiving of philosophical self-knowledge of knowledge as a substantial *Aufhebung* of all scientific knowledge of nature, culture, and history—as a return home, as it were, of the spirit from its exteriorizations and alienations in nature and history.

By this conception, Hegel overthrew the Kantian paradigm of a critical transcendental philosophy in the age of the empirical sciences and thereby understandably provoked the reaction of both nineteenth-century positivism and neo-Kantianism. But it must not be overlooked that Hegel's objective idealism, with its concept of the "objective mind," paved the way for a new awareness of the issues facing the human or cultural sciences (in German, *Geisteswissenschaften*), which after Hegel had to pose their own problems of a transcendental (viz. transcendental-hermeneutic) foundation.

The transcendental problems of hermeneutics eventually motivated the linguistic turn of First Philosophy in the twentieth century.[31] Of course, the linguistic-hermeneutic turn of phenomenology and cultural philosophy was supplemented by analytic philosophy, which was originally oriented toward symbolic logic and later developed into ordinary language philosophy. I think that Peircean "pragmaticist" semiotics and structuralist semiology were also among those streams of thought that inspired the novel paradigm of First Philosophy in the twentieth century.[32]

Consider Josiah Royce's final work, *The Problem of Christianity,*[33] which at least in Europe is still almost unknown. This work suggests a novel paradigm of transcendental epistemology, which I found while studying the understanding/explanation controversy concerning the methodological relations between the natural sciences and the humanities.[34] Here is the new paradigm in Royce's terms. In order to provide a foundation for scientific cognition, it is not enough to take recourse to the subject-object relation of representing the real, or of verifying hypotheses about the real, which has dominated modern epistemology; in addition, we have to take into account communicative understanding among the co-subjects of cognition (or among different stages of the same subject) in order to take into account the "nominal value" of the linguistic terms. It is in light of such nominal value that we must bring home the "cash value" of our knowledge.

To put this in my own terms, there is a fundamental complementarity of the subject-object relation and the subject-cosubject relation lying at the ground of all cognition.[35] We should recognize such complementarity not only for the epistemology of objectifying science, but also for hermeneutics. We must take into account the complementary presupposition of communicative understanding between the co-subjects of science; but also, when we engage in hermeneutics, we should not forget that when we attempt to understand other people—including the dead authors of classical texts—we are not objectifying them but rather communicating with them about something in the world. Therefore the novel paradigm of transcendental epistemology after the linguistic-hermeneutic turn could be labeled "communicative understanding about something" (in German, *Verständigung über etwas*).

But why do I call this a *transcendental* paradigm of epistemology, or even of First Philosophy? It is widely accepted in our time that the linguistic turn of philosophy in all its variants has undermined both metaphysics and transcendental philosophy in favor of all kinds of skepticism and relativism, the latter going along with inescapable insights into the dependence of our philosophical thought on a plurality of different—or even incommensurable—cultural traditions. That is why in the book *After Philosophy,* with my transcendentalism I figured as the white raven not only among the "end of philosophy" philosophers, but also (in a sense) among the representatives of a "transformation of philosophy."

This holds even when my position is compared with that of my friend Jürgen Habermas, with whom I share most of the structural features of a "universal pragmatics of language" and many tenets of "discourse ethics." But Habermas, though he sticks to the universality claim of the three (or, respectively, four) validity claims of argumentation, and sometimes even flirts with the idea of a "weak form" of transcendental pragmatics, thinks he has to reject the transcendental difference between philosophy and all empirical sciences and instead to defend a methodological unity between all "reconstructive" (social) sciences and philosophy.[36] Therefore he, like the Popperians, denies any aprioristic restriction of fallibilism and—here is the crucial point—does not shy away from claiming that in principle, the necessary presuppositions of argumentation (such as the four validity claims) have to be empirically tested just like the basic hypotheses of linguistic theories (for example, Chomsky's "innateness" thesis).

Therefore, Habermas must consider it possible, in principle, that the necessary presuppositions of argumentation may be falsified by—and yet at the same time presupposed as valid by—an empirical test. For the necessary presuppositions of argumentation are of course preconditions of any test whatsoever, just as they are necessary preconditions of meaningful talk about fallibility and falsification. Thus Habermas's position, too, involves a certain type of performative self-contradiction. The contradiction is rooted in Habermas's denial of the transcendental difference between the validity conditions of all empirical tests (in the widest sense) and the validity conditions of philosophical insights into those conditions. For, as I have emphasized already, though theses about the necessary presuppositions of argumentation are not immune to critique (as a dogmatic transcendentalism would suggest), the criterion of testing them does not lie in any possible experience but in the impossibility of disputing them without committing a performative self-contradiction. This is the specifically philosophical method of proving transcendental insights. Habermas ignores this insight of a transcendental pragmatics by demanding an empirical test for the presuppositions of argumentation, and he pays for this empiricist-scientistic fallacy by getting tangled up in performative self-contradiction; for he must, of course, in each empirical test actually presuppose what he wants to test.

I should add that I by no means reject the need for cooperation and mutual checking between philosophy and the reconstructive social sciences, which Habermas postulates in accordance with the tradition of the Frankfurt School of "critical theory." But, as I have pointed out in my attempt at a critical reconstruction of Lawrence Kohlberg's theory of moral development,[37] in such a critical cooperation both sides must use their own specific criteria of validation. Otherwise they will not be able to serve as critical partners of a mutual checking.[38]

The Philosophical Point of View after the End of Dogmatic Metaphysics

By discussing the Frankfurt School's query into the unity or difference between philosophy and the reconstructive social sciences, I hope to have displayed my conception of what the philosophical point of view after the end of dogmatic metaphysics amounts to. Here is a summary of my position.

Karl-Otto Apel

{ 174 }

1. By calling my conception "transcendental pragmatics" (at the beginning also "transcendental hermeneutics," and today also "transcendental semiotics"), I want to characterize a position of First Philosophy—theoretical as well as practical philosophy—after the twentieth-century linguistic-hermeneutic turn of philosophy.[39]

2. But in opposition to the skeptical and relativistic tendencies of today's philosophy, which apparently follow from the linguistic-hermeneutic turn, I stick to the ideas of First Philosophy and transcendental philosophy. By First Philosophy I do not mean the conception of ontological metaphysics which reigned from Plato and Aristotle until Kant, but a type of transcendental philosophy. But thereby, again, I do not mean the philosophy of the transcendental consciousness, which reigned from Kant through Husserl, but a novel type of transcendental philosophy after the linguistic-hermeneutic turn, a type that is both more restricted and more radical in its aprioristic claim to ultimate foundation.

2.1. In restricting the aprioristic claims of classical transcendentalism, I would follow, in particular, the transformation of Kantianism found in Charles Peirce's "pragmaticism."[40] This means that I would drop or at least relativize the whole constitutive apriorism of categorial schemes in favor of a transcendental pragmatic foundation for the validity of the laws of logic and the procedures of "synthetic inference" and "sign interpretation"; what grounds such procedures is the counterfactual anticipation, or regulative principle, of a necessary convergence— under ideal conditions—of these procedures toward an ultimate consensus in the "indefinite community of researchers." Along with this transformation of Kantianism, I endorse a sense-critical transformation of Kant's dualistic metaphysics (mere appearances versus unknowable things in themselves) into a conception of the "real" as the knowable that can never be known but would be the correlate of the "ultimate opinion."

2.2. The restriction of Kant's apriorism must go along with a radicalization of the transcendental claim to an ultimate foundation for philosophy. Peirce's foundation for the procedural laws of the semiotic logic of inquiry by the postulate of an ultimate consensus can and must be ultimately grounded by those presuppositions of argumentation that cannot be disputed without committing a performative self-contradiction. These presuppositions—for example, the four validity claims—can in fact be partially composed of the primordial consensus postulate of serious argumentation.

3. Thus, by strict transcendental-pragmatic reflection on the presuppositions of argumentation, a novel type of First Philosophy becomes possible that, in its kernel, does not contain any fallible hypotheses but only the indisputable conditions of fallible hypotheses. But the function of philosophy cannot and must not be restricted to that of a strictly transcendental First Philosophy. Since the speculative thought of human beings ought not to be restricted— even in the interest of the scope of empirical sciences— there should be a type of speculative, non-dogmatic, globally hypothetical metaphysics, as Peirce suggested. It could have its place between First Philosophy and the empirical sciences, providing the latter with seminal ideas for new paradigms of research, as philosophy in fact has done since the time of the pre-Socratics.

4. Finally, I should at least mention that the conception

Karl-Otto Apel

of transcendental-pragmatics as First Philosophy, in my opinion, can also provide an ultimate foundation for discourse ethics, and thereby for practical philosophy.[41] In this case, only two things can be grounded a priori: the normative preconditions of the procedures for ideal practical discourses, and a very formal principle of a history-related co-responsibility for shaping the institutional preconditions for (ideal) practical discourses. The rest—such as the determination of the material norms of ethics and of law, and eventually their application—has to be left to the practical discourses of the affected persons (or their advocates) and must be considered fallible and provisory.

Notes

1. In a similar way, I tried to answer the question concerning the meaning of "practical philosophy" or "ethics" to the audience of a broadcasting college in Germany in 1981. K.-O. Apel, D. Böhler, and G. Kadelbach (eds.), *Praktische Philosophie/Ethik: Dialoge* (Frankfurt am Main: Fischer, 1984), and K.-O. Apel, D. Böhler, and K. Rebel (eds.), *Praktische Philosophie/Ethik: Studientexte* (Weinhem: Beltz, 1984).

2. Immanuel Kant, *Critique of Pure Reason*, B833.

3. Ibid., B866–67.

4. K. Baynes, J. Bohman, and T. McCarthy (eds.), *After Philosophy: End or Transformation?* (Cambridge: MIT Press, 1987), 7.

5. Ibid., 18, n. 2.

6. Cf. G. Radnitzky, explaining the position of H. Albert, W. W. Bartley III, and himself in "In Defense of Self-Applicable Critical Rationalism," in *Absolute Values and the Creation of the New World,* ed. International Cultural Foundation (New York: International Cultural Foundation Press, 1983), vol. II, 1025–1069. Cf. also K.-O. Apel, "Fallibilismus, Konsenstheorie der Wahrheit und Letztbegrundung," in *Philosophie und Begrundung,* ed. Forum für Philosophie Bad Homburg (Frankfurt a.M.:

Suhrkamp, 1987), 116–211, reprinted in K.-O. Apel, *Auseinandersetzungen: In Erprobung des transzendentalpragmatischen Ansatzes* (Frankfurt am Main: Suhrkamp, 1998), 81–194.

7. It was elaborated in W. Kuhlmann, *Reflexive Letztbegrundung, Untersuchungen zur Transzendentalpragmatik* (Freiburg: Alber, 1985).

8. Cf. M. Niquet, *Transzendentale Argumente: Kant, Strawson und die Aporetik der Detranszendentalisierung* (Frankfurt a.M.: Suhrkamp, 1991).

9. Cf. R. Rorty, "The World Well Lost," *Journal of Philosophy* 69 (19), and "Transcendental Arguments, Self-reference, and Pragmatism," in *Transcendental Arguments and Science,* ed. P. Bieri et al. (Dordrecht: D. Reidel, 1979), 77–103. Cf. also Niquet, *Transzendentale Argumente,* 530ff.

10. Cf. R. Rorty, "Is Truth a Goal of Enquiry? Davidson Is Right," *Philosophical Quarterly* 45 (180), 281–300. Rorty also says: "We hope to justify our belief to as many and as large audiences as possible" (298). But how could he justify this hope or postulate? Considered in the light of his pragmatic theory of persuasion, the meaning of his postulate could lie only in a desire to increase the social success of persuasion, or else he had to take recourse to some claim to universal validity, which indeed would explain and justify the need to try out the force of the belief through unlimited attempts to reach consensus by arguments. Cf. J. Habermas, "Rorty's pragmatische Wende," *Deutsche Zeitschrift für Philosophie* 44 (5), 715–742.

11. Richard Rorty, "Universality and Truth" (unpublished manuscript, June 14, 1993).

12. Cf. Hilary Putnam, *Realism with a Human Face* (Cambridge: Harvard University Press, 1990).

13. See especially C. S. Peirce, "What Pragmatism Is," Coll. Papers, vol. 5, §§411–437; cf. 5.438ff, 5.453ff, 5.458, 5.460f, 5.497ff, 5.11ff. See also K.-O. Apel, *From Pragmatism to Pragmatism* (Amherst: University of Massachusetts Press, 1981), part II.

14. Cf. K.-O. Apel, "Fallibilismus, Konsenstheorie der Wahrheit und Letztbegrundung." I cannot here appropriately discuss recent objections against the meaningful use of regulative ideas as those concerning the conception of what the truth would be, objections that are in particular brought forward by A. Wellmer in *Ethik und Dialog* (Frankfurt am Main:

Suhrkamp, 1986), 91, and in "Wahrheit, Kontingenz, Moderne," in *Endspiele* (Frankfurt am Main: Suhrkamp, 1993), 162. I can only suggest here, that we misunderstand the regulative idea of the ultimate consensus if we derive from it the obligation of striving for a state beyond all possible communication. For such a formulation suggests itself only if we try to imagine what it would be to have reached the ultimate consensus under the conditions of history, or what it would be to reach a state beyond the end of human history. But this, I think, amounts to a hypostatization of a regulative idea which was forbidden already by Kant, who tried to de-Platonize this type of "ideas."

15. See J.-F. Lyotard, *The Postmodern Condition* (Minneapolis: University of Minnesota Press, 1984), 75.

16. Cf. K.-O. Apel, *Understanding and Explanation: A Transcendental-Pragmatic Perspective* (Cambridge: MIT Press, 1984), and "Types of Social Science in the Light of Human Cognitive Interests," *Social Research* 44 (3), 425–470, reprinted in *Philosophical Disputes in the Social Sciences,* ed. Brown (Brighton: Harvester Press, 1979), 3–50, and in K.-O. Apel, *Ethics and the Theory of Rationality* (Atlantic Highlands, NJ: Humanities Press, 1996).

17. Lyotard, *Postmodern Condition,* 8.

18. Cf. K.-O. Apel, "Plurality of the Good? The Problem of Affirmative Tolerance in a Multicultural Society from an Ethical Point of View," *Ratio Juris* 10 (2), 199–212, and "The Problem of Justice in a Multicultural Society: The Response of Discourse Ethics," in *Questioning Ethics: Debates in Contemporary Philosophy,* ed. Richard Kearney and Mark Dooley (London: Routledge, 1999).

19. Cf. Lyotard, *Tombeau de l'intellectuel et autres papiers* (Paris: Editions Galilée, 1984), 81, where he speaks of the "terreur rationalists (consensuelle) des philosophes d'origine parfois américaine mais surtout allemande."

20. My translation. Lyotard, *Le différend* (Paris: Editions de Minuit, 1983), 9. Cf. to what follows Manfred Frank, *Die Grenzen der Verständigung: ein Geistergespräch zwischen Lyotard und Habermas* (Frankfurt am Main: Suhrkamp, 1988).

21. Lyotard, *The Postmodern Condition*, 10ff.

22. Lyotard, *Le différend*, 162, 169, 172ff, 176, 182ff, 184, 186. Cf. K.-O. Apel, "Das Apriori der Kommunikationegemeinschaft und die Grundlagen der Ethik," in *Transformation der Philosophie*, vol. II (Frankfurt am Main: Suhrkamp), 358–436. An English translation is in Apel, *Towards a Transformation of Philosophy* (London: Routledge & Kegan Paul, 1980), and *Ethics and the Theory of Rationality* (Atlantic Highlands: Humanities Press, 1996).

23. Cf. K.-O. Apel, "Transcendental Semiotics and Hypothetical Metaphysics of Evolution: A Peircean or Quasi-Peircean Answer to a Recurrent Problem of Post-Kantian Philosophy," in *Peirce and Contemporary Thought*, ed. K. L. Ketner (New York: Fordham University Press, 1995), 366–397, reprinted in K.-O. Apel, *Toward a Transcendental Semiotics* (Atlantic Highlands: Humanities Press, 1994), 207–230.

24. Cf. Jürgen Habermas, *Der Diskurs der Moderne* (Frankfurt am Main: Suhrkamp, 1985), chapter 10.

25. Cf. K.-O. Apel, "The Challenge of a Totalizing Critique of Reason and the Program of a Philosophical Theory of Rationality Types," in *Reason and Its Other*, ed. D. Freundlieb and H. Hudson (Oxford: Berg, 1992), 23–48 (reprinted in Apel, *Ethics and the Theory of Rationality*, 250–274).

26. Cf. Habermas, "What Is Universal Pragmatics?" in *Communication and the Evolution of Society* (Boston: Beacon Press, 1979), 1–68. I have from the beginning interpreted "Universal Pragmatics," especially the four validity claims of argumentation, as a matter of "transcendental pragmatics"; see my arguments against Habermas's attempts at an empirization of the unavoidable presuppositions of argumentation in K.-O. Apel's *Auseinandersetzungen*.

27. Cf. my formula for ultimate grounding in "The Problem of Philosophical Foundation in the Light of a Transcendental Pragmatics of Language," in Baynes, Bohman, and McCarthy, *After Philosophy*, 250–290.

28. Cf. W. Kuhlmann, "Reflexive Argumente gegen den Determinismus. Zu Ulrich Pothast Die Unzulänglichkeit der Freiheitsbeweise," in *Sprachphilosophie, Hermeneutik, Ethik. Studien zur Transzendentalpragmatik* (Wurzburg: Konigshausen & Neumann, 1992), 208–223.

Karl-Otto Apel

29. Ludwig Wittgenstein, *Tractatus Logico-Philosophicus*, 6.45.

30. Cf. Hegel, *Phänomenoloqie des Geistes*, ed. J. Hoffmeister (Hamburg 1952), 63ff.; *Wissenschaft der Logik*, ed. G. Lasson (Hamburg 1966), vol. II, 496; *Vorlesunqen uber die Geschichte der Philosophie* vol. III, in Hegel's works (ed. Glockner) 19:555ff; *Enzyklopädie* (1830), § 10.

31. I think of the final work of Wilhelm Dilthey (Der Aufbau der geschichtlichten Welt in den Geisteswissenschaften," in *Gessamelte Schriften*, vol. 7, pp. 146f and 207ff. English translation in H. P. Rickman (ed.), *W. Dilthey, Pattern and Meaning in History*, London, 1961/New York, 1962, pp. 117ff. See also K.-O. Apel, "Wittgenstein and the Problem of Hermeneutic Understanding," in *Towards a Transformation of Philosophy*, London: Routledge & Kegan Paul, 1980, pp. 1–45, and Milwaukee, WI: Marquette University Press, 1998, pp. 1–45), of the linguistic-hermeneutic turn of phenomenology with Heidegger and Gadamer, and also of the hermeneutic application of Peircean Semiotics in the second volume of Josiah Royce's last work *The Problem of Christianity* (1913). Cf. K.-O. Apel, "Scientism or Transcendental Hermeneutics? On the Question of the Subject of the Interpretation of Signs in the Semiotics of Pragmatism," in *Towards a Transformation of Philosophy*, 93–135.

32. Cf. Apel, *Toward a Transcendental Semiotics*, and *From a Transcendental Semiotic Point of View* (Manchester: Manchester University Press, 1998).

33. Josiah Royce, *The Problem of Christianity* (New York: Macmillan, 1913).

34. Cf. Apel, *Understanding and Explanation*.

35. Cf. K.-O. Apel, "The Hermeneutic Dimension of Social Science and Its Normative Foundations," *Man and World* 25 (1992), 247–270, reprinted in Apel, *Ethics and the Theory of Rationality*, 293–315.

36. Cf. the characterization of Habermas's position in Baynes, Bohman, and McCarthy, *After Philosophy*, 291ff.; cf. also K.-O. Apel, "Fallibilismus, Konsenstheorie der Wahrheit und Letztbegrundung," and "Normative Grounding of 'Critical Theory' through Recourse to the Lifeworld? A Transcendental-Pragmatic Attempt to Think with Habermas against Habermas," in *Philosophical Interventions in the Unfinished Project of*

Enlightenment, ed. Axel Honneth, Thomas McCarthy, Claus Offe, and Albrecht Wellmer (Cambridge: MIT Press, 1992), 125–170.

37. Cf. K.-O. Apel, "Die transzendentalpragmatische Begrundung der Kommunikationsethik und das Problem der hochsten Stufe einer Entwicklungelogik des moralischen Bewußtseins," in *Diskurs und Verantwortung* (Frankfurt am Main: Suhrkamp, 1988), 306–369.

38. I found out, by the way, that Kohlberg, correcting himself, has confirmed this point for the relationship of philosophy and psychology. Cf. Lawrence Kohlberg, Charles Levine, and Alexandra Hewer, *Moral Stages: A Current Formulation and a Response to Critics* (Basel: Karger, 1983), 15ff.

39. Cf. K.-O. Apel, "Erste Philosophie hente?" in K.-O. Apel, Vittorio Hösle, Roland Simon-Schäfer, *Globalisierung: Herausforderung fur die Philosophie, Bamberger Hegelwochen 1997* (Bamberg: Universitätsverlag, 1998), 21–74.

40. Cf. K.-O. Apel, "Transcendental Semiotics and Hypothetical Metaphysics of Evolution," and "The Impact of Analytical Philosophy on My Intellectual Biography," in *From a Transcendental-Semiotic Point of View* (1998).

41. Cf., on the one hand, J. Habermas, *Moralbewusstsein und kommunikatives Handeln* (Frankfurt am Main: Suhrkamp, 1983), *Erläuterungen zur Diskursethik* (Frankfurt am Main: Suhrkamp, 1991), and *Faktizität und Geltung* (Frankfurt am Main: Suhrkamp, 1992), where the claim to ground morality by transcendental reflection on the discourse principle has been definitely dropped since the latter has been declared to be "morally neutral"; cf., on the other hand, K.-O. Apel, *Ethics and the Theory of Morality, Diskurs und Verantwortung,* and *Auseinandersetzungen,* where the last three essays contain my critique and alternative proposals with regard to Habermas's conception of practical philosophy.

Karl-Otto Apel

Contributors

KARL-OTTO APEL is professor of philosophy at Johan Wolfgang Goethe University, Frankfurt am Main. His publications include *Transformation der Philosophie* (1976), *Towards a Transformation of Philosophy* (1980), *Die Erklären: Verstehen-Kontroverse in transzendentalpragmatischer Sicht* (1979), *Understanding and Explanation: A Transcendental-Pragmatic Perspective* (1984), *Collected Essays*, vols. I and II (1994, 1996), and *From a Transcendental Semiotic Point of View* (1998).

ROBERT BRANDOM is Distinguished Service Professor at the University of Pittsburgh. His publications include *Rorty and His Critics* (2000), *Making It Explicit* (1994), and *Articulating Reasons* (2000). He is currently writing a book on Hegel.

KARSTEN HARRIES is professor of philosophy at Yale University. His publications include *The Meaning of Modern Art: A Philosophical Interpretation* (1968), *The Bavarian Rococo Church: Between Faith and Aestheticism* (1983), and *The Ethical Function of Architecture* (1997).

SARAH LILLY HEIDT is assistant professor of philosophy at the John Jay College of Criminal Justice of the City University of New York. She has published essays on Hegel and on phenomenology.

{ 183 }

MARTHA C. NUSSBAUM is Ernst Freund Distinguished Service Professor of Law and Ethics at the University of Chicago, with appointments in the Philosophy Department, the Law School, and the Divinity School. Her publications include *Love's Knowledge: Essays on Philosophy and Literature* (1990), *The Fragility of Goodness: Luck and Ethics in Greek Tragedy and Philosophy* (1986), *Sex and Social Justice* (2000), and *Women and Human Development: The Capabilities Approach* (2000).

C. P. RAGLAND is a graduate student in philosophy at Yale University. He has published articles on Duns Scotus and on the contemporary realism/antirealism dispute.

BARRY STROUD is Mills Professor of Metaphysics and Epistemology at the University of California, Berkeley. His publications include *Hume* (1977), *The Significance of Philosophical Scepticism* (1984), *The Quest for Reality: Subjectivism and the Metaphysics of Colour* (1999), *Understanding Human Knowledge* (2000), and *Meaning, Understanding, and Practice* (2000).

ALLEN WOOD is professor of philosophy at Stanford University. His publications include *Kant's Moral Religion* (1970), *Kant's Rational Theology* (1978), *Karl Marx* (1981), *Hegel's Ethical Thought* (1990), and *Kant's Ethical Thought* (1999). He is also the general co-editor of the Cambridge edition of the works of Immanuel Kant.

Index

consensus: Lyotard's heterogeneity of language games, 161–64; morality in context of, 164; truth in context of, 158–59, 178*n10*

context-dependence, universality and, 159

Copernican theory, 69

counter-metaphysics, 165–66

critical thinking, philosophy and, 112–16, 155–56

criticism, of concepts, philosophers' duties regarding, 77–78, 86–87

Critique of Pure Reason, 62, 168–69

culture: apologetic *vs.* analytical questions and, 100–101; heterogeneity of language and, 161–64; philosophy and, 28–31; public philosophy and, 127; things that have history and, 74–75. *See also* multiculturalism; relativism

d'Alembert, Jean le Rond, 103

Danto, Arthur, 51

Davidson, Donald, 154, 156

Derrida, Jacques, 15, 18, 154, 158; end of philosophy discussed by, 164–66

Descartes, René, 62; certainty as concern of, 79; on freedom of will, 65

development economics: criticisms of, 128; feminism and, 137; phi-

losophy and, 9–10; public philosophy and, 122–47

diagnostic philosophy, characteristics of, 41

Dickie, George, 51

Diderot, Denis, 104, 113–14, 119*n9,* 120*n13*

dignity, public philosophy and concept of, 138–39

Dilthey, Wilhelm, 181*n31*

Directory of American Philosophers, 52

discourse ethics: philosophy and, 2, 6, 15–16; transcendental pragmatics and, 172–74, 177, 182*n41.* *See also* meta-discourse

discursive practice, application of concepts and, 84

doctrines, philosophy and, 31–33, 37–38

dogmatic metaphysics, end of philosophy and, 168–69, 174–77

domestic violence, public philosophy and, 122–23, 136–37

Dostoevsky, Fyodor, 60

Dumarsais, César Chesnau, 104–16, 119*n9,* 120*n10*

Dummett, Michael, 84–87, 154

economics: public philosophy and, 9, 130–31, 133–47; quality of life and, 126–47. *See also* development economics empiricism: public philosophy and, 135–47; rationalist critique of, 83–84; understanding and knowledge in context of, 82–83

Empiricism and the Philosophy of Mind, 19–20, 83–84

Encyclopedia Britannica's Book of the Year, 56

Encyclopédie, ou Dictionnaire raisonné des sciences, des arts et des métiers, par une société des gens des lettres, 103–7, 118n5, 119n9, 120n10

end of philosophy: Derrida's discussion of, 164–66; Foucault's discussion of, 165; as goal of philosophy, 62; Lyotard's discussion of, 161–64; metaphysics and, 156–57; transcendental argumentation and, 158–77

Enlightenment: critique of philosophy by, 111–16; Foucault on, 115–16; Kant's concept of, 101–4, 112–16; meaning of philosophy and, 96, 101–4; philosophical concepts of, 13, 16–17

entitlement, judgment and action in context of, 78–79

epistemology, transcendental paradigm of, 171–77

Ethical Functions of Architecture, The, 59

ethics: philosophy and, 11; professionalization of philosophy and,

57–60; toolbox approach to philosophy and, 57–60. *See also* morality

Ethics (Spinoza), 53

evaluative concepts, circumstances and consequences of applying, 85–86

experience, role of, in public philosophy, 135–47

explication, *vs.* analysis, 77

facts, role of, in philosophy, 33–34

fallibilism, pragmatics and, 155, 172–74, 176–77

family: justice and structure of, 136; public philosophy and role of, 139–40

feminism: international issues facing, 137; Kant's practical postulate and, 147; public philosophy and, 121–47

First Philosophy, Abel's concept of, 168–77

formal concepts, conditions of truth and, 88

Foucault, Michel, 15, 18; criticism of Enlightenment by, 102, 118n4; on end of philosophy, 154; end of philosophy discussed by, 165; on Enlightenment, 115–16

Foundations of the Metaphysics of Morals, 65–66

Frankfurt, Harry, 47–49, 52, 63

industrialization of philosophy, 51–52, 54–56

industry, ethics and philosophy applied to, 58–60

inferences: application of concepts and commitment to, 88–89; concepts and defects in, 86–87; judgments as application of concepts and, 83; material inferences, 87; philosophy as examination of, 4

institutional theory of philosophy, 51, 54

intellectualism, philosophy in context of, 107–11

internal capabilities, philosophy and investigation of, 132, 149n13

James, Henry, 135

James, William, 143, 158

Jaspers, Karl, 53–54

judgment, Kant on concepts and, 78–81

justice issues: philosophy in context of, 9, 15–16; public philosophy and, 125–27, 135–47; resource distribution and, 136–47

Kant, Immanuel, 16; on concepts, 78–80, 92–93; consciousness discussed by, 90–91; on end of philosophy, 62; Enlightenment discussed by, 101–2, 112–16; "four questions" of, 153; on freedom, 65–67; *Gelehrten* concept and, 112–16; Hegel's critique of, 170–71; Lyotard's critique of, 163–64; metaphysics in work of, 168–71, 175–76; practical postulate of, 146–47; public philosophy and work of, 133; on reason and judgment, 161–62; "scholastic" *vs.* "worldly" concept of, 153; "self-consistency of reason," 156; on wisdom and philosophy, 110–11

Kierkegaard, Søren, 49

knowledge: reasoning and, 82; *vs.* understanding, 20, 76–77

Kohlberg, Lawrence, 174, 181n38

language: application of concepts and, 83–84; argumentation and, 157–58; discourse ethics and, 172–74; Lyotard's postmodernism and, 160–64; meta-discourse in context of, 162–64; public philosophy and role of, 134–35, 143–47, 150n17

Law of Peoples, The, 136

Lebensraum in philosophy, 55–56

Le différend, 163

legal structure: in India, 150n21; wealth maximization as goal of, 142

Leibniz, Gottfried, 169

Lessing, Gotthold, 49

Levinas, Emmanuel, 5

observable concepts, circumstances and consequences of applying, 85–86
ontological metaphysics, 169
origins of philosophy, 62–63
Oxford English Dictionary, 57

paintings, painters on, 26–27, 35
patronage, philosophy and role of, 30
Peirce, Charles, 160, 171, 175–76
persuasion, argumentation and, 157–58
Philosophical Investigations, 60–61
philosophy: canon of work in, 34–35; characteristics of, 1–22; contemporary developments in, 8–9; economics and, 9–10
Philosophy and the Mirror of Nature, 69–70
physics, philosophy of, 118$n7$
Pindar, 64
Plantiga, Alvin, 69
Plato: apologetic *vs.* analytical questions and, 99–101; Hegel's discussion of, 171; metaphysics and work of, 175; on philosophy, 7–8, 63–65
poetry, apologetic *vs.* analytical questions and, 100–101
policy making, role of philosophy in, 132–33, 141–47
politics: production of capabilities

and role of, 149$n13$; public philosophy and, 131–47
Popper, Karl, 159
postanalytic philosophy, characteristics of, 17–18
Postmodern Condition, The, 161–63
postmodernism: concepts of philosophy in, 15–16; "end" of philosophy and, 18; public philosophy and, 127, 148$n4$; regulative idea and, 160–64
power, meta-discourse in context of, 162–64
practical philosophy: Kant's practical postulate, 146–47
pragmaticism, argumentation and, 160, 175
pragmatics: fallibilism and, 155; philosophy and, 10–12, 143–47; transcendental argumentation and, 158–59, 175–77, 178$n10$; validity claims of argumentation, 166–69. *See also* utilitarianism
precedent, rational tradition and, 76
Principia Mathematica, 37, 118$n6$
Problem of Christianity, The, 171–72
productivity, in philosophy, 50–52
professionalization: agenda enlargement and, 54–55; end of philosophy and, 154–55; ethics

in context of, 57–60; legitimacy of philosophy and, 2–4, 10; niche identity in philosophy and, 37–38; of philosophy, 30; standards in philosophy and, 52–53; teacher *vs.* genuine philosopher and, 50–51

progressive thinking, Enlightenment and, 116

property rights, public philosophy and issues of, 138–47

publication and publishing: concept of philosophy and, 2; productivity in philosophy and, 50–51

public image of philosophy, 56, 154

public philosophy: characteristics of, 8–9; international feminism and, 121–47

Putnam, Hilary, 154

quality, professionalization of philosophy and, 52–53

quality of life: core concepts of, 130–31; economic and philosophical debate concerning, 9–10; human capability as measurement of, 135–47; plural metric assessment of, 148n5; public philosophy and, 125–47

questions, apologetic *vs.* analytic questions, 98–101

Quine, W. V., 36–37

Rameau's Nephew, 113–14, 120n13

rationality: counter-metaphysics and, 166; freedom of will and, 65–67; nature of things and history of things and, 75–76; normative assessment and, 90–92; philosophy and, 12; response as application of concept in, 82–83; understanding *vs.* knowledge and, 77

Rawls, John, 136, 143

reality: criterion of truth and external realism, 159–60; metaphysics and, 169; scientific truth and, 70–71

reason: action in context of, 105–7; application of concepts and, 82–84, 93–94; experience and, 83–84; Kant on consistency of, 170–71; philosophy and, 12, 103; theories concerning, 111

regulative ideas: criterion for truth and, 160, 178n14; postmodernism and, 160–64

relativism: public philosophy and, 127–28, 134–47, 148n4; pursuit of truth and, 68–71

religion: apologetic *vs.* analytical questions and, 99–101; philosophy and, 31

repression, philosophy in presence of, 29

Republic, 99

social sciences, public philosophy
and, 128–29, 148n8
Socrates: apologetic *vs.* analytical
questions and, 99–101; Plato's
description of, 64, 70–71; public
philosophy and influence of,
129–30, 132–33, 141–42,
149n9
Socratic spirit, philosophy in context of, 1–2, 10
space of reasons, 82
speculative metaphysics, philosophy and, 2, 6, 15–16
speech act theory, argumentation
and, 157–58
Spinoza, B., 53
stimuli, capacity for response to,
82–83
Strawson, Peter, 156
Stroud, Barry, 2–8, 10–11, 16–18,
20; definition of philosophy, 25–
46
"systematic" transformation of
philosophy, 154–55

Taylor, Charles, 150n17, 155
teaching, genuine philosophers
and profession of, 50–51
teamwork, impact on philosophy
of, 53
Thales of Miletus, 100
Theaetetus, 64
theory of philosophy, doctrines
and, 38–39

therapeutic philosophy, characteristics of, 40–43
toolbox view of philosophy, 56–
60
Tractatus, 53, 169
transcendental pragmatics, Abel's
concept of, 155–58, 166–77,
180n26, 182n41
truth: commitment to, in philosophy, 52, 63–64; conditions of,
88 89; consensus theory of,
158–59, 178n10; philosophy in
context of, 48–49; science *vs.*
philosophy and pursuit of, 67–
71

überreden concept, 157–59
überzeugen concept, 157–59
uncertainty, philosophical problems and, 61–62
understanding: apologetic *vs.* analytical questions and, 100–101;
vs. knowledge, 20, 76–77; reasoning and, 82
universalism: context-dependence
and, 159; philosophy in context
of, 15–16; public philosophy
and, 127–28, 135–47
university: philosophy and role of,
29–31, 97–98; philosophy in
curriculum of, 132–33
utilitarianism, public philosophy
and, 127–28, 133